PICTORIAL MILESTONES OF
MANCHESTER CITY FOOTBALL CLUB

FROM
MAINE MEN
TO
BANANA CITIZENS

by GARY JAMES
and
the late KEITH MELLOR

Published by

 TEMPLE  PRINTING

Nottingham
England

MCMLXXXIX

Price £6.95

ISBN 1 870010 08 6

FOREWORD BY JOE MERCER, O.B.E.

Manchester City supporters have always been loyal. They have supported the Club during the good times and bad. I will never forget the way they welcomed the team back from each of our cup successes in the late sixties and early seventies.

The supporters helped to make my time as Manager of City one of the most enjoyable and successful periods of my life.

This book has been put together by my good friend Keith Mellor and a young Kippax season ticket holder, Gary James. Keith had previously published a number of footballing books and had the experience, whereas Gary had never been involved with publishing before. The two of them spent many months preparing and researching.

The book looked as if it would have to be cancelled when Keith was, sadly, taken ill and passed away. Keith's enthusiasm had encouraged Gary at the start and it was because of this that everybody connected with the book wanted it completed. Since then, although the work was difficult Gary has completed the book and has produced one of the most interesting productions around.

All City supporters, and followers of football in general, will find something to interest them with photographs and cuttings from the 1880's to the present day.

I hope you enjoy this book and I am grateful that I have been involved with one of the finest clubs in the country.

THE STORY OF ST. MARK'S, WEST GORTON, ARDWICK A.F.C. AND MANCHESTER CITY F.C. 1880-1989

The Club's early history adapted from "Association Football and the Men who made it" (1905) Caxtons and Newspapers of the time.

The acorn of the Manchester City oak was as puny a thing as could be imagined. Planted in soil that was perhaps too virgin, its attempts to grow were pitiable, till one day the husbandmen transplanted the sprout. Even then it refused to grow into anything worthy of its race, and years of careful nurturing were necessary ere the tree came to be noticed.

Probably Manchester City is not alone in its struggles; most great things have insignificant births, and it is to be doubted if any First Division club has ever attained to prominence without battling through years that have a habit of seeming black and unpromising. But in these days when every town or city is incomplete without its great football organisation, there is room for wonder that Manchester allowed so much time to slip away without obtaining a representative club in the elect circle of Soccer. It is the more wonderful because in other branches of sport the city of cotton has in its time provided the cream — nay, it has produced its champions galore.

It seems strange, but it is nevertheless true, that Manchester City only became a First Division team in the season of 1899-1900. In that season they went by no means so badly, finishing seventh; but they were thrown back into the Second Division at the end of the season of 1901-2; and it was not until another period in the second section had been experienced that they won their way back. They stayed there and won the national Cup, a feat which puts them abreast of the best clubs that ever played.

The statistician would probably tell you that Manchester City possesses the record among clubs for trouble. It has indeed in its day passed through a host of afflictions; some undeserved, others "asked for". It seems to have been doomed from its inception to a curse of so-called reorganisation, and hardly a season has come that has not brought with it alarms or actual war in its own camp.

But let us hark back to the details of the club's early life. It was in 1880 that, in the face of predominant Rugbyism, a few "Soccer" enthusaists, attending St. Marks' Church, formed a club under the title of West Gorton. After playing close to the present City Ground for a short time, a hire of the Kirkmanshulme Cricket Ground was obtained, some miles away. But they were not allowed to stay long; the cricketers objected to the ploughing up of the ground, and the order to quit went forth. That was the death knell of West Gorton.

Out of the ashes rose Gorton Association Club in 1884, but here again failure came early. Not till 1887 did the enthusiasts, nothing daunted by the records of past futility, revive the spirit of "Soccer" in the district. Then they called the club Ardwick, and the ground at present in use by the City was secured on a short lease.

This was in 1889, and the promoters having obtained the services of several amateurs, thought to increase the chances of advancement by the engagement of one professional. He — it was J. Hodgetts — was employed at the princely salary of 5 shillings a week.

Soon came the inevitable raid of the Scottish preserves. There journed South in 1890, Douglas, a goalkeeper from Dundee, and David Weir, of

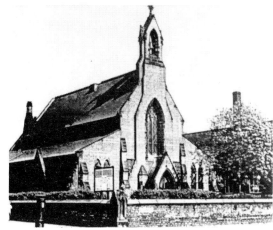

St. Mark's (West Gorton) F.C. was formed by two church wardens at St. Mark's Church, Clowes Street, West Gorton. The first ground was a rough patch on Clowes Street.

Lawrence Furniss played for Gorton from 1884-1887 when an injury ended his career. He then became more involved within the club. He was Secretary during the early 1920's and President when the club won the League in 1936-37.

Maybole. It seemed after this that the club was at least on the highway to the desired goal, and the winning of the Manchester Cup in April 1891 by a point to nothing was looked upon as the real beginning of an onward march that was to take them at least half-way over the land that lay between them and the Leaguers.

Probably on the strength of this success they were admitted to the Alliance in the season of 1891-92. With them then was Dave Russell. Seventh was their position at the end of the season, and they won the Manchester Cup again, this time beating Bolton Wanderers by four goals to none, when the latter had the assistance of such men as Sutcliffe, Somerville, and "Di" Jones.

The merging of the Alliance in the Second Division of the League saw Ardwick among the chosen. Their first season was successful enough, finishing as they did fifth on the list; but in the session of 1893-94 they fell from grace, sank to the thirteenth position (unlucky number!), and from want of financial stability went out of existence.

From that day the strenuous stalwarts of Manchester Association football went forward with a mission that accounts for the City Club being where it is now. To Mr. Joshua Parlby must be given the credit for its resurrection and for the early organisation which set it on its legs again. But he had with him some sturdy devotees, and though finance was more than an uncertainty, the Manchester City Football Club, Limited, was floated, and on 1st September 1894 the first match was played, Bury defeating the Manchester team by 4 goals to 2.

It was with the inception of Manchester City that Meredith, the famous right-wing Welshman came into prominence. It was probably his presence in the team that accounted for the scoring of a record number of goals for that season's competition – 82. The club finished ninth in the Second Division, and in the following season they only missed the championship by virtue of an inferior goal average. The season of 1895-96 was a memorable one, seeing that they made 46 out of a possible 60 points, and were not once beaten at home. In the play-off for the championship at Hyde Road on Good Friday 1896, they were beaten by Liverpool, and the only satisfaction they got was half of the £798 "gate".

In the succeeding season Manchester City finished sixth on the list, but in 1897-98 they came within an ace of joining in the rewards that awaited the two top clubs. A defeat at Newcastle put them into third place, and so it was not till the following season that they crossed the bridge to the First Division.

They went into the First Division side by side with Glossop North End, Bolton Wanderers and Sheffield Wednesday being the displaced teams. Finishing seventh and eleventh in the first two seasons in premier class, the Manchester City Club struck a vein that set the whole of Lancashire football students wondering. The club finished absolutely last on the table, having scored only 28 points. Relegation to the Second Division ranks, of course, was a consequence. The organisation had been allowed to drift into a very lax condition, and the work of pulling the club round was by no means easy. Indeed, but for the timely aid of Mr. Edward Hulton, the City Club might not now be in existence.

A new secretary, Mr. T.E. Maley, brother of the famous "Willie" Maley, of Glasgow, was obtained, and with the new directors he set to work to put "his house in order."

The crowning glory came to the club when the English Cup was won in the season of 1903-04. Here they beat in succession Sunderland, Woolwich Arsenal, Middlesbrough, Sheffield Wednesday, and in the final Bolton Wanderers by 1 goal to 0. In that competition they scored 12 goals against 3.

Perhaps no players have had more to do with Manchester City's success since the last reorganisation than Burgess, the Glossop-cum-Manchester International back; Hynds, a typical raw-boned Scot; Hillman, among the greatest of goalkeepers; Frost, a white-haired youth who was rejected as a forward and became a noted half-back; and perhaps most famous of all Meredith, the pride of Wales and of Hyde Road.

4

EARLY CLUB GROUNDS

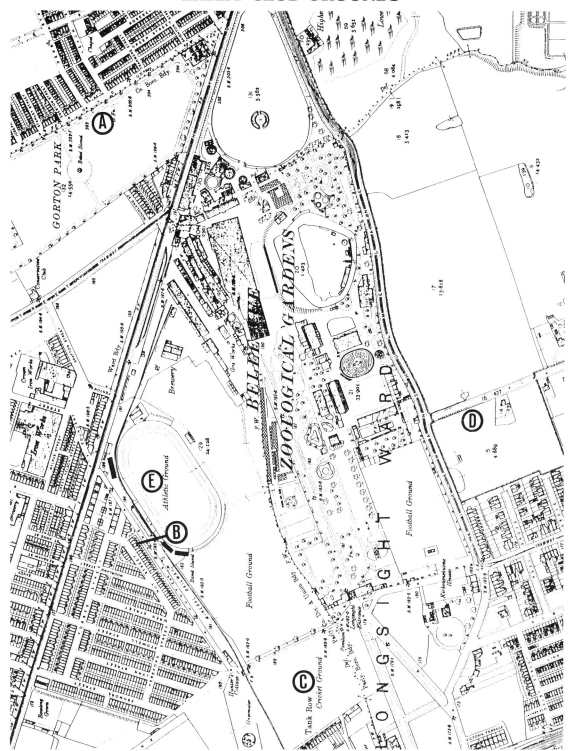

From the Godfrey Edition of Old Ordnance Survey Maps, Lancashire Sheet 104. 16, showing Gorton and Belle Vue 1905.
A: Queen's Road Ground, 1882-83. B: W. Meredith's house in Nut Street. C: Kirkmanshulme Cricket Club Ground, 1881-82. D:
Pink Bank Lane Ground, 1884-85. E: Belle Vue Ground, site of the 1889 floodlit game between Ardwick and Newton Heath.

HURST CLARENCE V. ST. MARK'S, WEST GORTON.

The above clubs met for the first time this season to play a game of football (association rules) on Saturday last, on the ground of the latter. The weather was very fine, which brought a good number of spectators to witness the game, which proved to be a friendly one. The home team chose the way to play, which was a little down hill, but not much. The visitors put the ball in motion, which was kept in play for some time when the visitors got a corner kick which proved successful for them, as they scored from it. The home team then put the leather about, both teams showing some good play, nothing more being done until half-time was called. Half-time the home team put the ball in motion, the visit of it now put two more goals to the list, that team three goals to the bad. Time being out pleasant games ended in favour of Clarence nil. Teams: Hurst Clarence—J. Hindle, J. Barton, backs; J. Dickin (captain), a: backs; E. A. Lees, H. Bickerton, J. P. ... Turton, and A. R. Adams, forwards. St. goal; W. Sumner (captain) and E. Greve and A. Macdonald, half backs: W. C... Downing, R. Millard, R. Hopkinson, and Umpire, J. E. Bickerton.

NEWTON HEATH (L. Y. 2) V. WEST GORTON.

This match, under Association rules, was played at Newton Heath on Saturday last, and, after a pleasant game, resulted in a victory for the home team by three goals to nil. Two goals were scored for Newton Heath in the first half, one by J. Jones, the other being put through the West Gorton goal by one of their own backs whilst attempting to stop a shot from E. Thomas. E. Thomas also kicked a goal in the second half. The following were the teams: West Gorton—Kitchen, goal; Sumner and Hopkinson, backs; Greves and ... half backs; Beastowe and Pilkington, right wings; McDonald and Chew, centre... ...d and Pervor, left wings. Newton Heath—Shaw and Morris, backs; R... y and Fulton, rs and Latham, right wings; Thomas and J. Hopwood and Edwards, left wings

WEST GORTON (ST. MARK'S) V. BENTFIELD, GREENFIELD.
ASSOCIATION RULES.

These clubs met to play their return match at Longsight on Saturday last, both sides being fairly represented West Gor... ... to play up hill with a slight breeze, ... elected to press the visitors, the result h... were registered during the first half, both be... Hopkinson. After change of ends the home be a... mile several attacks on the home goal, but ... managed to equalise matters, both goals... Bradbury. The home team during third ... siderably, but not played with renewed ... the visitors' goal claimed a free kick, ... was again successful in kicking the ... ...ing further was scored, and ... ...ng ... team by three goal... ... ...al; Sumner (c... ...al;... and McK... ... a...

HURST V. ST. MARK'S, WEST GORTON (ASSOCIATION RULES).

This match was played on Saturday last on the ground of the former, at Hurst, in very stormy weather. The visitors won the toss, and elected to play with the wind in their favour. The home team kicked off, taking the ball close to the visitors' goal, when Lawton, dashing in, shot the ball between the posts. The visitors kicked off from the centre and after a little give-and-take play in midfield, the home forwards again came away, and, not to be denied, Lawton scored goal No. 2. Shortly after this half time was called. Ends having been changed, they which with two goals to the bad and a strong wind against team, kicked off. During the second half the visitors were hard pressed, and many shots were made at the visitors' goal, but the wind carried them wide of the mark. Ultimately the visitors' forwards getting possession made a good run, and Lomas, the Hurst ousted h... had to run out to save his charge, kicking the ball, which b... nded from one of the visitors close to the Hurst goal, but ... mick of time came to the rescue, and the visitors took two a corner, but nothing ... the visitors had to act on the defen... ...al of time Axon scored the third goal. ...aying the ball had been over the goal pre... saw this, and the visitors kicked Time was now called, having the goals, one disputed, to nil.

HURST V. ST. MARK'S, WEST GORTON (ASSOCIATION RULES.)

This match was played on Saturday, on the ground of the latter at Longsight, it being the return match. The ground was in a very sloppy state, and consequently the falls were very numerous. The home captain won the toss, and elected to play with the ground in his favour. Lawton kicked off with a gentle touch to J. Firth, and the home goal was soon in danger. W. C. Firth took the corner, and landed the ball well in front of the uprights, and Berry being on the spot scored goal No 1. The home team kicked off, but the visitors backs were equal to the occasion, and quickly returned the ball into mid field, and the forwards made for the home goal, but its keeper ... ... his charge well, and got the ball away, but only for a short time, as, for the second time, Berry scored from a beautiful header. No other point was made up to half time, and one home team, with two goals to the bad, kicked off, but they could make no headway. The visitors' forwards were working together like machinery, scoring goal after goal in such a rapid manner that at the call of time they were the winners by seven goals to love. The following were credited with scores: Berry 2, Ingham (captain) 2, Lomas 2, and one to a home player. Teams—Hurst: Goal, J. Hodgins; backs, Knott and M... dn; half backs, W. C. Firth and T. Ingham; right wing, Berry and Hartley; left wing, Lomas and Ingham (captain); centre, J. Firth and J. W. Lawton; umpire, J. Goddard, Esq. St. Mark's: Goal, Cooper; half backs, Sumners (captain) and Keats; half backs, Greaves and Smith; forwards, Kitchen, McDonald, Pilkington, Harroway, Hgss, and another.

Newspaper reports taken from "The Ashton Reporter" from the Club's first season, including the first ever meeting between Manchester United (then Newton Heath) and Gorton.

FROM GORTON

TO ARDWICK

Above: The Hyde Road Hotel, Ardwick, the birthplace of Manchester City Football Club. The gates on the left of the Hotel once led directly into the Bennett Street football ground, the Ardwick Club's first ground. The Club also used the Hotel for meetings.

Right: The same building today, called the "City Gates" for a short period before closing down in 1988.

Below: A convincing victory for Ardwick during their first season. One of the goal-scorers, Jack Hodgett was the Club's first professional. He was paid 5 shillings per week in 1887.

ARDWICK v. HYDE. — (Ardwick District Charity Cup, second round). — At Ardwick. Hyde kicked off. Ardwick scored first from the toe of Drinkwater, and from the kick off they took it down and scored again. Then Parker scored for Ardwick, and all the first half Ardwick pressed. On change of ends, with wind in their favour, it was thought that Hyde would press, but it was not so. Parker, Hodgetts, and Callagan scored, and from Manning, at half back, Callagan scored. Then Hyde scored one. McKenzie afterwards scored the eighth for Ardwick, the result being :—

ARDWICK .... 8 goals.
HYDE .... 1 „

1889 FLOODLIT CHARITY MATCH

*In January 1889 the Hyde coalmine
explosion resulted in the death of twenty-
three miners. Newton Heath agreed to
play an Ardwick team under floodlights for
the explosion fund. The game was played
at Belle Vue, Manchester on 26th
February 1889.
Newton Heath 3 Ardwick 2.*

NEWTON HEATH v. ARDWICK DISTRICT

This match was played at Belle Vue Gardens
last night before a tremendous crowd, the "gate"
being for the benefit of the Hyde Explosion Fund.
There were twenty of the Wells's lights round the
ground, but still there seemed to be some
difficulty in seeing the ball at times, especially
when it was off the ground. It was stated
that there had been quite 6,000 tickets sold, and
the gates were crowded for over two hours before
the time for starting, so that there would be quite
10,000 people present, and it ought to result in a
considerable addition to the fund. Mr. Charles
Jennison kicked off, and R. G. Barlow was referee.
The game was not a success as an exhibition of
football, but still at times there was some good
bits of play, which were applauded by the spectators,
who seemed to be quite enthusiastic. The chief
feature of the match was the cheering when
the ball was kicked either over the bar or outside,
as most of the spectators were sure it went
through. The scoring done was four goals by
Newton Heath and one by the District, but, unfortunately for the former, one of theirs was put
through his own goal by Powell. Score:—Newton
Heath, three goals; Ardwick and District, two
goals.

*The Ardwick team that day included a few guest players.
The teams were:*
*ARDWICK AND DISTRICT: F. Leather (Ardwick)—Goal; G. Seldon
(Denton) and E. Bower (Ardwick)—Backs; W. Watmough, K. McKenzie
(Ardwick) and T. Davies (Hyde)—Half Backs; J. O'Brien, J. Stanley
(Ardwick), J. Williams (Hyde), J. Connolly (Denton) and C. Bolton (West
Manchester)—Forwards.*
*NEWTON HEATH: T. Hay—Goal; J. Powell and J. Mitchell—Backs; T.
Burns, J. Davies, and J. Owen—Half Backs; W. Tait, J. Gothridge, J.
Doughty, G. Owen and R. Doughty—Forwards.*

1891
MANCHESTER CUP WINNERS
ARDWICK 1 NEWTON HEATH 0

The 'Cambridge' Blues of Ardwick won the Manchester Cup for the first time in April 1891 by beating rivals Newton Heath 1-0 at the ground of "The West Manchester Club".

DAY, APRIL 19, 1891.

MANCHESTER CUP.—Final Tie.

Newton Heath v Ardwick.—The meeting of Newton Heath and Ardwick in the final for the local cup has caused probably more interest than in any of the previous six, and there would be about 10,000 spectators present on the West Manchester ground. It was rather unfortunate that the big Rugby match between the Champion County and the Rest of England was fixed for the same day, but the officials made the best of it by kicking off rather later than usual. The two clubs are now keen rivals, but in the three meetings this year Newton Heath have won twice, whilst the other game was spoiled by the fog, and ended in a draw. The following gives the results of the two clubs for the present season :—

	Pl.	W	D	L	Goals For	Agst
Newton Heath						
Ardwick						

The Heathens have met rather stronger opponents, and also have played more away from home. In the previous rounds Ardwick have beaten Denton and West Manchester, whilst their opponents have drawn with Hurst and beaten Stockport County, the former game being awarded them on account of Hurst declining to play on gates settled by the Association. Weir started the game for Ardwick, who at once got well down, and gained a corner, which was taken and well placed by Bennett. The ball was got out of danger and Milarvie got on a splendid run, but was badly fouled by Bennett. Ardwick got away with a nice run, and Weir scored with a long shot seven minutes after start. The Heathens now got away several times, but their shooting was bad. Ardwick left wing got well down, and from a free kick the ball was put through, but owing to nobody having touched it, "no goal" was ruled. The teams this very even, each comedian having in be called upon to defend his charge. The Heathen forwards now got away with a short run, and Bennett was again prominent with his rough play, fouling and hurting Craig that it was necessary to stop the game a few minutes. The players were now all called together and cautioned for their rough play. Ardwick now got down, and Lambie caused Slater to fist out a good shot. Close to half-time the Heathens gained a fruitless corner, and tried hard to equalise, but could not succeed. At half-time the score was as follows : Ardwick, 1 goal ; Newton Heath, nil. On restarting the game the Heathens went away, and gained a corner, which was well placed by Sharp, but Owen kicked out. Harman was next prominent with a good run, and was fairly pulled up when close in. Ardwick now had a turn, but Davies put the ball outside. Lambie now put in one which hit the crossbar, and soon after a corner fell to Ardwick. The Heathens played a game absent in combination. The Heathens now gained a corner, which was taken by Farman, and Ramsay had hard lines in not equalising. Slater was now called upon to have a splendid shot from Weir, which he did in safe style. The Heathens next got away, but Sharp ran it out. "Marde" close in the Heathens goal looked very dangerous, but the ball was got out of danger. Five minutes from finish Milarvie got in a good run, and was grandly stopped by Robson. During the remainder of the game the Heathens had hard lines in not equalising, and when the whistle blew Ardwick ran out the winners of the Cup for the first time in their career. Final :

ARDWICK	1 goal
NEWTON HEATH	Nil

[EM]PIRE, SUNDAY, AUGUST 31, 1890.

[Em]pire Football Review.

[OF TH]E COMING SEASON.

Who Will Win, and Who Lose in 1890-91.

[COMPRE]HENSIVE GLANCE [ROUN]D THE COUNTRY

[ALLIAN]CE CLUBS (*Concluded*).

[A SP]ECIALIST in LEATHER.

[In a compre]hensive glance around the country last week beyond the limits [a]nd Alliance clubs, and several [som]ewhat tardy correspondents, [compre]hensively glanced at what is [with]out these organisations, have [w]ith further details. Without, [want]ing to speak further of these [and] acknowledgment, I hasten [in] resting body of clubs forming [M]IDLAND LEAGUE.

[Ra]ngers, the one representative of [las]t year's Alliance, naturally had [th]e way in which they cut up, and [mi]ght more into contact with the

OTHER LANCASHIRE CLUBS.

The Ardwick Club have a thoroughly good working committee, who, besides retaining the whole of last season's players, have enlisted a regular cohort of powerful players, all of good standing. The team now on the spot is made up from the following :—

Douglas (Dundee Our Boys), Leather, and Warman, goal ; Robson (Ayr), Haydock (Bolton Wanderers), Bennett, Head, backs ; Milne, McWhirter, Whittle, Pearson (Bolton Wanderers), Weitnough, "Jones," half-backs David Weir (captain), Rushton (Bolton Wanderers), Campbell (Ayr), McWalrine (Ayr Athletic), McColl (Burnley), Haworth, Hodgetts, O'Brian, forwards.

There will also be three new players from Scotland, all of whom have signed the professional form. McColl, who had signed for Burnley, it will be noticed, has been released by them. The ground has been re-turfed, drained, and otherwise improved to the tune of over £600, and its central situation, surrounded by railways and trams, warrants the outlay. The public of Manchester have been judiciously catered for by the arrangement of a very strong list of home fixtures, and many more of the Ardwick big gates are looked forward to. In view of Ardwick's bold bid for the supremacy of Manchester, the three matches with Newton Heath and the two against West Manchester will be very instructive. Matches with the Bolton Wanderers, Blackburn Rovers, West Bromwich Albion, Derby County, and Accrington are already on the list, while the executive expect other League clubs at Ardwick during the season.

A preview of the 1890-91 Season proved to be correct when it stated that Ardwick were aiming to be Manchester's premier team.

1891-92 THE "BREWERYMEN" RETAIN THE MANCHESTER CUP AND ENTER THE ALLIANCE LEAGUE.

THE ALLIANCE.
Results up to date :—

	Pld.	Won.	Lost.	Drn.	For.	Agst.	Pts.
Notts Forest	13	10	1	2	46	12	22
Newton Heath	11	8	1	2	32	14	18
Sheffield W'day	13	7	4	2	38	21	16
Small Heath	11	7	3	1	28	16	15
Burton Swifts	12	5	5	2	27	33	12
Ardwick	12	3	6	3	24	32	9
Bootle	12	4	7	1	24	37	9
*Birm'ham St. G.	14	4	8	2	30	34	8
Lincoln City	9	4	4	0	15	26	8
Walsall T. Swifts	10	3	7	0	11	33	6
Grimsby Town	8	1	5	2	14	19	4
Crewe Alexandra	9	3	6	0	13	29	-1

* Two points deducted for playing ineligible men.

Ardwick v. Newton Heath. — This, the "Derby" match at Hyde Road, was expected to help the brewery men materially—financially speaking. The dry weather of the last few days had decidedly improved the appearance of the ground, and a fine afternoon caused the spectators to roll towards Hyde Road in very large numbers. The pay boxes placed outside were literally besieged, and at two o'clock there would be 5000 or 6000 present. When play started this number had increased to 10,000 or 11,000. The men turned out punctually, when it was seen that Macfarlane, the Heathens' captain, was unable to play, Denman taking his place as right full back. Ardwick played a new acquisition in Cook, from the defunct Midland League Club. Referee, Mr. Hall, of Crewe. Mr. George Scott, of the Palace of Varieties, set the ball rolling towards the visitors' goal, and Donaldson made tracks, Robson robbing him. A throw in to Newton followed, and Farman caused Douglas to fist away in the first minute. Sharpe did a bit of neat work, the ball eventually going out. Hands against Clements gave Ardwick a look in, and a big shot by Robson caused Turner to fist away. Another free kick to Ardwick was headed out, and Sharpe followed with a fine run, which Denman stopped. The first corner fell to Newton, but it was cleared, and a splendid bit of work by Davies and Milne ended in the latter scoring after nine minutes' play. A foul was awarded against Morris, but Cook saved, and Sharpe was tripped when in a good position to shoot. The home team were playing a grand defensive game, Cook giving the Heathens another corner, followed by a second, which Owen sent wide. Hood gave Douglas a handful, but he got it away, and corners again fell to Newton. Sharpe got well away again, but Denman was in the way, and Stuart, at the other end, shot over. A moment later Farman failed to reach the ball, which he rushed out, and a foul was given against Stewart for pushing. The ball was put through by Sharpe, but the whistle having blown, no score followed. Slater just saved, Milarvie dashed up, and Douglas at the other end got the leather away grandly. After several good attempts, Farman got in a beauty and equalised, both Robson and Jackson missing the ball previously. Sharpe was hurt and had to retire at this period. Donaldson sent in a good shot, which shaved the posts, Sharpe received a cheer for coming on again, and Slater neatly caught a flying shot from him. Hands against Seldon relieved the home goal momentarily, but Farman got in, and with a fine swift shot put on the second goal for the Heathens. Clements next saved a smart attack by Milarvie and Sharpe. Half-time score — Newton Heath, 2 goals; Ardwick, 1. The second half was soon resumed, and before a few minutes had elapsed, the Ardwick goal was threatened, but Douglas, who was performing grandly under the bar, saved in a marvellous manner, and fully deserved the hearty recognition of the crowd. From a subsequent goal kick, Milarvie and Sharpe, who were playing by far the best of the forwards, made tracks towards the visitors' goal, and Milne equalised, a feat which was followed by the waving of hats and loud cheers. With only a quarter-of-an-hour to play, the excitement ran high. Newton Heath never allowing their opponents to cross the half-way line, but the home defence came out of the ordeal grandly and prevented further downfall. Final :—

NEWTON HEATH .... 2 goals
ARDWICK .... 2 "

Right: A report of the Manchester Senior Cup Final played at the home of Newton Heath at North Road, Clayton. Ardwick beat Bolton Wanderers 4-1 on 23rd April, 1892 to retain the Cup. Ardwick had defeated Heywood Central 3-1 away in the first round on 13th February. Their next opponents in the semi-final were Fairfield at Hyde Road. Ardwick won this game 4-0 on 12th March.

Left: Over 11,000 supporters went to Hyde Road for the 'Derby Match' with rivals Newton Heath. The game resulted in a 2-2 draw with Ardwick's goals coming from J. Milne the former Bolton player. Ardwick finished the season in twelfth place.

MANCHESTER SENIOR CUP.
(FINAL TIE.)
BOLTON WANDERERS v. ARDWICK.

The above competition reached the final stage when Ardwick (holders) met Bolton Wanderers, on the Newton Heath ground at North-road. This is the first time the Wanderers have appeared in the final for this cup, as they only entered at the beginning of this season. In former years the result of the competition was practically a foregone conclusion, as Newton Heath won the cup year after year ; but the rapid strides made by Ardwick put more interest into the affair, and last year they managed to beat the "Heathens" by 1 goal to nothing. This is the first time since the competition was started that Newton Heath have not appeared in the final. In the preliminary encounters Ardwick had to meet Heywood Central and Fairfield, whilst the Wanderers have beaten Stockport County and Newton Heath. Both teams put forth their best eleven for the match under notice, and it was not surprising that a fast game was witnessed. The Ardwick committee have had their team training at Matlock, whilst the "Trotters" have done what they required at home. The game was not started until 4.5. There would be about 8000 spectators present, when Cassidy started the ball for the Wanderers against a stiff wind. Ardwick at once took up the running, but Milarvie when hard pressed put the leather into touch. The ball was then worked down, but Robson took care of Bentley, and his goal went wide by several yards. The goal-kick afforded some relief, and Sutcliffe had to use his hands to a capital shot from Milne. The ball still hovered in close proximity to the Bolton goal, but Davies at length put the ball wide of the uprights. The Bolton forwards by some nice passing got the leather away, but Middleton intervened, and Sutcliffe had to save a slow shot from Milarvie. The Ardwickites, assisted by the wind, were playing a good game, and Jones was compelled to give a corner. The ball was well placed, but Parry came to the rescue, and Cassidy missed the mark by the nearest possible margin. The Wanderers then assailed, and Douglas, in saving a shot from Bentley, was compelled to give a corner, but nothing resulted. Munro now had a capital chance, but instead of rushing away he sent the ball to the centre. Milne here got the leather, and the Ardwick forwards rushed away, but Sutcliffe by some splendid play prevented them from scoring. A free kick to Ardwick followed, but Gardiner was successful, and with a tall kick transferred the ball to the opposite end, but the Ardwick backs were in excellent trim, and cleared time after time. The Ardwickites got away again, and Sutcliffe only just saved a shot from Milne by giving another corner, but the kick did not result in anything. Just as the whistle was about to be blown Munro scored through a miskick by Robson. The Ardwick forwards at the restart rushed up, and Morris made the score 1 each, which was the score at half-time. After the interval, Milne restarted the ball for Ardwick, and Bentley immediately shot into touch. The play, on the restart, was again in favour of the Wanderers ; but the defence of the Alliance team was grand. Robson, with a beautiful kick, got the leather away. Weir, getting the ball at the centre, evaded all his opponents, and beat Sutcliffe with a beautiful shot, which was greeted with loud and prolonged cheering. This reverse put the League team on their mettle, and Douglas had to be on the alert to keep his goal intact, and after several attempts, Bentley put the ball high over the bar. Ardwick then broke away and gained a free kick close to the Bolton goal. Weir took it, and Milne tipped the ball past Sutcliffe. On restarting, the Boltonites went at it more determined than ever, but Ardwick were not to be beaten, and kept them well in hand. The Alliance team again went away, and Milarvie putting the ball across, Weir notched the fourth. The Wanderers now played like a beaten team, allowing their opponents to run round them. Ardwick, though, had certainly the best of matters during this half, playing against the wind with surprising energy. Cassidy now forced his way through several opponents, but Robson intervened and cleared. Time was at length called. Ardwick gaining a decisive victory. Final :—

ARDWICK .... 4 goals
BOLTON WANDERERS .... 1 "

A boy's season ticket for the Club's very first season in the Football League.

ARDWICK FINISH FIFTH IN DIVISION TWO, 1892-93

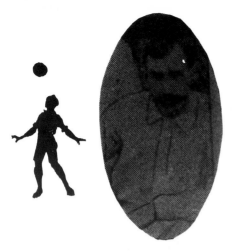

Left: R. Milarvie made 17 appearances for the Club and scored 8 goals in the Club's first season in the league.

Below: Comment and report of the first matches of the season.

Ardwick have been busy getting their house in order for next Friday, when they open the season with a second team match. McVickers, Steel, and Stono are expected to sign within the next few days, and by Monday or Tuesday the whole team will be in "strong work." We understand the negotiations for the formation of the club into a limited liability company are making satisfactory progress, and altogether the prospects of the club are brighter than for some time past.

Below: Comments regarding the collapse of Ardwick A.F.C. and the formation of Manchester City Football Club.

Football affairs out Ardwick way have become considerably mixed, and the supporter of the game in that district at present "dunno where 'e are." So far back as last October the club had got into such low water that it was found necessary to call a meeting of the ticket-holders to discuss the situation, and they decided to carry on the club somehow or other till the end of the season, when it should be allowed to die.

These proceedings, it is fair to assume, met with the approval of the committee, since that body do not appear to have made any protest. In fact, if our information be correct, the committee have not met since the middle of October last until quite recently.

Meanwhile, a few of the ticket-holders and others had made up their minds to start a new organisation at the end of the season, to be called The Manchester City Football Club Company Limited, and on Wednesday last they made application for affiliation to the Lancashire Association. That body, we are informed, is prepared to grant the request on production of an agreement showing that the new club has a ground to play up in. The ground the promoters have in view is the Ardwick enclosure, and they say that the landlords, the Manchester, Sheffield and Lincolnshire Railway Company, will sign the necessary document within the next few days.

About that, however, there is a doubt. The members of the Ardwick committee have once more taken in hand the reins of management, with Mr. Allison at their head, and they announce their intention of making a determined effort to reconstruct and carry on the old concern. Therefore, there are two applicants for the ground, and on whichever party gets it will doubtless depend the decision of the Lancashire Association.

SECOND DIVISION.

Results up to date :—

	Pld.	Won.	Lost.	Drn.	For	Agnt.	Pts.
Small Heath	1	1	0	0	4	1	2
Ardwick	1	1	0	0	7	0	2
Sheffield United	1	1	0	0	4	2	2
Burton Swifts	1	1	0	0	7	1	2
Darwen	1	1	0	0	2	1	2
Grimsby Town	1	1	0	0	2	1	2
Bootle	1	0	1	0	0	7	0
Walsall T Swifts	1	0	1	0	1	2	0
Lincoln City	1	0	1	0	2	4	0
Crewe Alexandra	1	0	1	0	1	7	0
B'rol'm Port Vale	1	0	1	0	1	2	0
N'thw'ch Vict'ria	1	0	1	0	1	2	0

Ardwick v. Bootle.—Despite the fact that the weather was of an unpromising character, rain falling nearly the whole of the time, there was an attendance numbering 4000 persons on the Ardwick ground, when these teams decided their first League match. Ardwick started the game for Ardwick, who by some good forward play, well backed up by Russell, immediately assumed the aggressive. A fine dribble by Law, the visiting centre, neutralised matters. Then Hopkins passed grandly to Davies, who got away with a clear field; but with only McLaughlin, the goalkeeper, to pass, he shot miserably. The play ruled in favour of the visitors for some time afterwards, and on one occasion Douglas got the ball away with quite half a-dozen men surrounding him, after which Davies took a fine pass from Morris and dodged round Ardlie, but the ball struck the upright. The visitors then attacked in a mild sort of way, Douglas saving his charge twice, following which Angus was fouled by Hutchison, for which a penalty kick was allowed, but Russell shot into McLaughlin's hands. Shortly afterwards, however, Weir dribbled grandly, and, passing when near goal to Morris, the latter equalised. From this point to the interval the play was of a most one-sided description, Ardwick playing their opponents to a standstill, and Davies scored the second and fourth, Middleton third, ... the home team failing by the last member to nil at the interval. Law started the second half, and a complete bombardment of the Bootle goal ensued, Morris eventually securing the next goal, and after a momentary visit to the Ardwick quarters during which Douglas was tested with a shot from Finlayson, the Bootle goal had several narrow escapes of a further downfall, Weir on one occasion just missing his mark, while on another McLaughlin saved in fine style. The visitors' left then broke away, and Douglas had to deal with shots from Gallagher and Law, but a minute later Law on scored the seven's for the home team, as the result of some good play on the left by Milarvie. The visitors, who played a little better towards the finish, were inferior at all points to their opponents, and were most decisively beaten. Final :—

ARDWICK .... 7 goals
BOOTLE .... Nil!

FROM
ARDWICK A.F.C.
TO
CITY

The annual meeting of the Football League has been held, much talking indulged in, and the business done is practically nil. Like the House of Lords, the League hates reform like poison, and will have none of it. Thus the absurd rule as to a two-thirds majority remains in force, neither the First nor Second Divisions are to be extended, and the farcical test games are to be continued. Hence it is a case of as we were, and next football season, therefore, will be witnessed the anomalous spectacle of the English Cup winners figuring among second-class clubs.

ARDWICK A.F.C. 1894-95
Back row, left to right: W. Iles (Trainer), A. McDowall (Full Back), G. Hutchinson (Goalkeeper), Mr. W. Skerratt (Assistant Secretary), Mr. W. Chapman (Chairman), J. Lumsden (Half Back).
Middle row: F. Dyer (Full Back), H. Smith (Half Back), W. Bowman (Half Back), E. Douglas (Half Back), A. Bennett (Full Back).
Front row: H. Tomkinson (Right Wing), T. Johnston (Inside Right), J. Nash (Centre Forward), G. Ballantyne (Inside Left), R. Milarvie (Left Wing).

THE FORMATION OF MANCHESTER CITY F.C.

We are not much surprised at the rejection of the extension scheme. Aston Villa, Sunderland, and other influential clubs have always opposed any extension; and it was hardly to be expected, as we said some weeks ago, that the Second Divisioners would submit quietly to the loss of their most attractive fixtures.

The inclusion of the English Cup-holders, and the substitution of Manchester City, Bury, Leicester Fosse, and Burton Wanderers for Ardwick, Northwich Victoria, and Rotherham, should make the Second Division games much more attractive next season than they were last, and accordingly a corresponding increase in the size of the gates.

For the four vacant places in the Second Division there was keen competition, no fewer than nine clubs making application for admission—viz., Manchester City, Leicester Fosse, Bury, Burton Wanderers, Blackpool, Loughborough, Accrington, Rossendale, and Rotherham Town. Of these, Manchester City and Leicester Fosse tied for first and second places, and Bury and Burton Wanderers "dead-heated" for third and fourth.

The confidence shown by the League in the Manchester City ought to materially help the officials of the new club in raising all the capital they require. We understand that plenty of good men are applying for positions, and all that is wanted is a little more money. The sooner that is forthcoming and the stronger the team will be, and, consequently, the more certain the prosperity of the club. As will be seen from an announcement elsewhere, the share list is still open.

Mr. Parlby, the new secretary of the Manchester City, headed the poll for a place on the management committee, and Mr. Starling—who last year was the other representative of the Second Division—was replaced by Mr. Strawson, of Lincoln City. Messrs. Lewis and Molyneux represent the First Division on the management committee. The other officers elected were Messrs. J. J. Bentley, president; Mr. L. Ford and Mr. E. Browne, vice-presidents; and Mr. H. Lockett, secretary.

So far the promoters of the new Manchester City Football Club have met with encouraging support, many applications for shares coming in from people who have not hitherto supported the game in Ardwick district with their purses. People who find it inconvenient to attend the bank during the ordinary hours of business may send in their applications to any of the directors, who will forward them to the proper quarter. In reply to several inquiries we may state that it is proposed to appoint Mr. Parlby secretary, whose influence in the football world should prove a great benefit to the club.

We are pleased to hear that the opposition to the Manchester City Football Club has been abandoned, and that the way is now clear for the new club to get a fair start. The promoters of the new organisation held a public meeting on Thursday, and, judging from the crowded attendance, and the enthusiasm of those present, the Manchester City Football Club should obtain plenty of support.

Charlie Williams was the City goalkeeper between 1894 and 1902. He made a total of 232 appearances for the Club before signing for Tottenham. He was born in Welling in 1876 and died in South America in 1952.

1894 MANCHESTER CITY'S FIRST SEASON

MANCHESTER CITY 1894. Back row, left to right: J. Prowse, R. Milarvie, D. Robson, C. Williams, F. Dyer, J. Broad.
Centre: J. McBride, H. Bowman, T. Chapman, M. Clifford, G. Mann.
Front: T. Little, J. Marples, W. McRedoe, A. Rowen, P. Finnerhan, W. Meredith.

The Manchester City Football Club have this week secured M. Calvey, the centre forward of Blackburn Rovers. He played for them in about half the League matches and all through the Cup ties. He is a fine young fellow, who learned his football in the army. He has weight and youth on his side, and should make a big name for himself. R. Jones, the centre half of the Everton Combination team, has also been engaged. He has often taken the place of Holt in League matches. He is a finished player, placing the ball with great judgment, and is a very hard worker. H. Smith, the right full back of Blackpool, has recently thrown in his lot with the new "City" club, and comes with a big reputation well earned. From the foregoing it will be seen that Mr. Parlby and his colleagues are doing their utmost to secure a strong team, but their efforts would be all the more successful if the general public hurried along with their applications for shares. The terms on which these shares can be had should suit everybody.

The 'Umpire' 3rd June 1894. A review of the 'City' clubs first signings.

Pat Finnerhan was brought to City from Northwich VIC. He made a total of 89 appearances for the Club between 1894 and 1897 and scored 27 goals.

1899 CHAMPIONS OF DIVISION TWO

ENGLISH LEAGUE v. IRISH LEAGUE

This Inter-League match was played on the ground of the Manchester City Club, and despite the depressing weather which prevailed, some 15,000 or 16,000 persons witnessed the play. The Irish team, which was supposed to be a strong one, had undergone three alterations; while on the English side, Williams (West Bromwich) was displaced by P. Homfrey, of Gainsborough, at back. A local feature of interest was the inclusion in the English team of Williams and Holmes, of Manchester City, and Bryant, the outside right of Newton Heath. The teams were:-

IRELAND - Lewis (Glentoran), goal; Parvis (Glentoran) and Foreman (Cliftonville), backs; Jack Pyper (Cliftonville), Milne (Linfield), and McMaster (Glentoran), half backs; Darling (Linfield), McArthur (Glentoran), James Pyper (Cliftonville), Kelly (Glentoran), and Alex. Campbell (Cliftonville), forwards.

ENGLAND - Williams (Manchester City), goal. Earp (Sheffield Wednesday) (captain) and P. Homfrey (Gainsborough Trinity), backs; Booth (Blackburn Rovers), Morren (Sheffield United), and Holmes (Manchester City), half backs; Bryant (Newton Heath), Bloomer (Derby County), Beats (Wolverhampton Wanderers), Wheldon (Aston Villa), and Schofield (Stoke), forwards.

Referee: Mr. Marshall, Glasgow

The Englishmen, in white jerseys and blue knickers, first made their appearance shortly before three o'clock, followed a little later by the Irish players, who figured in green jerseys and white knickers. A little preliminary practice, and Earp and Milne met in the centre of the field to toss for choice of ends. Milne won the toss, and Beats kicked off for England. The play at once opened with plenty of excitement. In warding off an attack by Milne, Booth miskicked, and the ball went into the English goal, but Williams saved in good style. Then came some smart attacks by the representatives of England, and following a fine run and centre by Bryant, Lewis saved a couple of smart shots, but a moment or two later Bloomer notched the first point, and a little later Schofield the second point for the Englishman. Thus five minutes' play yielded a couple of goals to the home country, who got through again, but offside was successfully claimed. The visitors then came away in a body, but Earp came to the rescue, and Holmes kicking across to Bryant, that player made good use of the opportunity. Morren put in a tremendous amount of work, and one of his passes to Bryant ended in the Newton Heath man sending splendidly across the goal, for Wheldon and Schofield, however, to miss the chance. The pace had slackened a little by this time, but nevertheless the attacking was monopolised by England, the Irishmen rarely breaking away. Once, however, they did, and James Pyper sent out to Darling, who sent just by the upright. The wearers of the green again forced their rivals back but Alec Campbell sent over the line as the result of some play in which combination was not a conspicuous quantity. England pressed again, when Lewis saved a slow shot from Bloomer, following which the Irishmen had a chance of clearing their lines had not McMaster handled. Some pretty combined work by the English forwards was then witnessed, and on two occasions Wheldon shot over, with capital opportunities for scoring presenting themselves, but the Villa representative eventually made up somewhat for his previous shortcomings in the shooting line by scoring England's third goal with a low shot which Lewis could not reach. Previous to this some spirited play by the sons of Erin resulted in P. Homfrey and Earp being placed in an exceedingly tight corner, but Darling put an end to the chance by shooting wide. Just before the interval Beats added the fourth goal for England, who thus led at half-time by 4 goals to nil. James Pyper restarted, and the play at once went in favour of England. Bloomer put in a long shot which skimmed the bar. Jack Pyper then beat Holmes, who sent along to Darling, and that player dashed away and then shot. Several of the Irish forwards closed in on Williams, who, however, cleared splendidly from Kelly. Play after this went in the vicinity of Lewis when Wheldon missed scoring with an open goal, but after some give-and-take work and a fine piece of combination by Bryant and Bloomer, from which Beats just missed scoring, Schofield put the ball past Lewis for the fifth time, Ireland appealing unsuccessfully. The Irish right wing again troubled their opponents' defence, Holmes, however, clearing the English lines in grand style, amid the

intense cheering of the crowd. A few seconds later Bloomer had scored again for the home country, a sprinting down the ground he let fly some twenty yards from goal, through which the ball travelled at a tremendous rate and gave Lewis no chance of saving whatever. Booth put in some very effective work, but was eventually outdone by the Campbell, who with a long drooping shot opened the scoring for Ireland. A lot of desultory play at the visiting country's end followed, but relief came to the Irishmen through Earp falling. Kelly got away and then transferred to Alec Campbell, who gave to Darling, Booth, however eventually bringing relief to the defenders, for whom Wheldon presently scored the seventh goal as the result of a fine pass by Bryant. Lewis covered himself with glory by saving from Bloomer as the ball came through a crowd of players, but a moment or two later the Irish custodian was beaten for the eighth time by Beats as the result of a flying shot. Final:

> ENGLISH LEAGUE .... 8 GOALS
> IRISH LEAGUE .... 1 GOAL

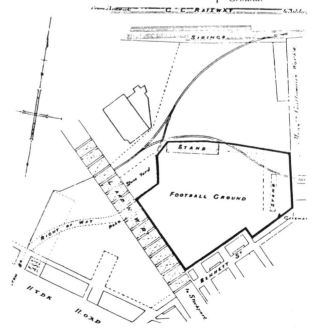

Left: November 1897. The League v. Irish League at Hyde Road.

The Second Division Championship winning team of 1898-99. Manchester City and local rivals Glossop North End were the first teams to gain automatic promotion into the first division. Previously the teams would have been involved in a series of Test Matches. Below: A plan of the Club's Hyde Road Ground.

NOTTINGHAM FOREST v. MANCHESTER CITY

FOOTBALL PLAN OF FIELD

Football League Match—FOREST v. MANCHESTER CITY

City Ground, Nottingham, Dec. 27, 1899

REFEREE—Mr. COOPER, Blackburn

C. H. RICHARDS, PRINTER, (Owner of Copyright)
Lower Parliament Street Nottingham.

Colours—Forest, Red

FOREST   FOREST

REGISTERED   COPYRIGHT

Allsop

Right side]   Peers   Iremonger   [Left side

Frank Forman   McPherson   Norris

Fred Forman   Calvey   Beveridge   Morris   Capes

Williams   Dougal   Gillespie   Ross   Meredith

Holmes   Smith   Moffat

Left side]   Jones   Read   [Right side

Williams

MANCHESTER   MANCHESTER

.......goals

The Official Nottingham Forest programme for the game against City on 27th December 1899. Forest won by two goals to nil.

MR. A.J. BALFOUR VISITS HYDE ROAD 29th SEPTEMBER 1900

Blackburn Rovers v. Manchester City. — Blackburn Rovers opened the season at Ewood Park with their first League encounter against Manchester City, hitherto only regarded in Blackburn as doughty Cup opponents. There were 8000 spectators. The Rovers played the same eleven as last season, with the exception of Crook for Briercliffe, at inside right, while the City had no alteration whatever. Booth won the toss, and Referee Stott started the game promptly, the Rovers having advantage of the wind. The Rovers were first to get away, aided by a foul against Ross for pushing. Hurst dropped a lovely shot into the City goalkeeper's hands, which he threw away nicely. Again the Rovers' centre players got away, but Smith intercepted the final pass and a foul against Houlker put the Rovers on the defensive momentarily. Booth relieved, but Ross, getting hold, bothered the home defence until Houlker ran the ball out. Bad kicking by Bar let the Rovers in again, but Jones came to the rescue and cleared finely. The City right took up the running, and, well fed by Ross, Meredith dropped a lovely centre in front of the Rovers' custodian, who just scraped the ball away at the cost of a fruitless corner. Hulse initiated a fine run down the middle of the ground, the City defence being well beaten; but Williams scooped up the ball and threw behind, the resulting corner being abortive. A quarter-of-an-hour from the start Meredith scored a splendid goal for the City, after Ross had tried and failed. Less than a minute afterwards the Rovers equalised from a free-kick taken by Brandon. The Rovers continued to press amid growing excitement. A series of fouls gave the City relief, but the Blackburn men came back, and Hulse with the goal at his mercy shot past the corner. Hurst followed by netting the ball from an offside position, the point being promptly disallowed. Then the City right cleared away, and Meredith passing to Ross, that player shot in, the visitors claiming that Thompson had failed to properly clear, and the referee allowed them the goal amid loud hooting. For some time the Manchester men held the upper hand, their right wing being almost irresistible, but the Rovers got away at last, Blackburn heading over. Another splendid run by Meredith and Ross brought the home custodian out of his goal, disaster being narrowly averted. Several desperate attempts by the Rovers' right wing were coolly met by the City defence, but a grand shot by Hulse deserved to score. The City goal was fairly bombarded for some time, but towards the interval the game opened out, although the Rovers still pressed hard for the equalising point. Ross was frequently cautioned by the referee for a legal infringement of rule. Half-time: — Manchester City, 2 goals; Blackburn Rovers, 1 goal. The second half opened with the Rovers again attacking, the final effort being entrusted to Hurst, who shot dreadfully wide. The visitors retaliated on the left wing, but Dewal shot wildly. Hulse was brought down by Hay, but, after a short stoppage, was able to resume. A free kick put into goal by Brandon was finely fisted away by Williams, and the City right wing again attacked Meredith, hitting the upright with a smart attempt. A run by the Rovers' right wing was spoiled by Williams' bad centre, but ten minutes from the re-start the game was equalised from a free kick, the ball being rushed through by Hurst and Blackburn after the City goalkeeper had played it. Aroused by this City played up strongly, but Gillespie was penalised for throwing the Rovers' custodian after he had cleared. The home side then came again, and amid cheers strove hard for the lead. As the end approached the pace slackened somewhat, both sides suffering from the heat. The City right forced a corner off Booth, but it was fruitless. Several other attempts, mainly by the centre and right, came to nothing but at last E. Williams got his head to a fine cross by Meredith, and again put his side ahead. Five minutes afterwards the score was again equalised, Hurst beating the City custodian at close quarters after Brandon had dropped in a free kick, the game continued to be evenly contested. Seven minutes from the finish Crook took a centre from Hurst in the air, and put the Rovers ahead with a beautiful shot amid terrific cheering. The Rovers continued to press up to the finish, the City seldom breaking away. Final: —

Prime Minister Mr. A.J. Balfour, Member of Parliament for East Manchester, visited the newly refurbished Hyde Road ground in September 1900. Here Mr. Balfour is inspecting a typical refreshment bar served by Chesters Brewery. Chesters Brewery had provided a great deal of financial assistance in the Club's early years in exchange for exclusive rights to sell their products at the ground. Local Brewer Stephen Chester Thompson had persuaded Mr. Balfour to become a patron of the club in the early 1890's.

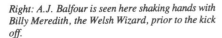

A report of City's first game in the First Division on 2nd September 1899. Meredith scored City's first goal after 15 minutes. The result was Blackburn 4 City 3.

Right: A.J. Balfour is seen here shaking hands with Billy Meredith, the Welsh Wizard, prior to the kick off.

1902-03 CITY PROMOTED AS CHAMPIONS

CHANGING PLACES.

SAD FATE OF BOLTON & GRIMSBY WHO SINK INTO THE "SECOND DIVISION"; & PLEASING PERFORMANCE OF MANCHESTER CITY & SMALL HEATH WHO GAIN THE COVETED SHORES OF THE "1st DIVISION".

Following City's relegation in 1901-02 the Club was determined to bounce back at the first attempt. Which they did. During the season City played 34, won 25, drew 4, after scoring 95 goals they finished first with 54 points.

Below: Tom Maley was appointed Secretary of City during the close-season of 1902 following the Club's relegation from Division One.

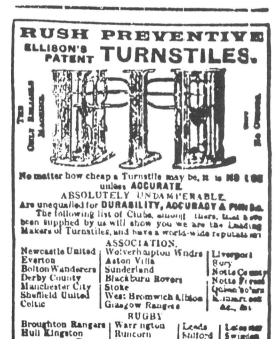

1903-04 RUNNERS-UP IN THE FIRST DIVISION AND THE CLUB'S FIRST "ENGLISH" CUP SUCCESS

A PEEP INTO FUTURITY.

Some day, perhaps, in the far, far distant future, when most of us are dead and gone, Manchester City and Bury may be able to decide as to which of them is most entitled to the possession of the Manchester Senior Cup. The "Daily Dispatch" published a cartoon on their series of drawn games, and we have taken the liberty of reproducing it.

MANCHESTER CITY FOOTBALL CLUB.

WINNERS OF ENGLISH CUP, 1903-4.

RUNNERS-UP. FOOTBALL LEAGUE, 1903-4. • JOINT HOLDERS MANCHESTER CUP, 1903-4.

CITY'S MARVELLOUS START TO THE SEASON

City won the first four games of the season beating Stoke (A) 2-1, Derby (H) 2-1, Wolves (above) (H) 4-1, and Notts County (A) 3-0.

City's magnificent season continues when on 7th November 1903 they beat local rivals 3-1 in the race for the League Championship.

"UMPIRE" FAVOURITES.

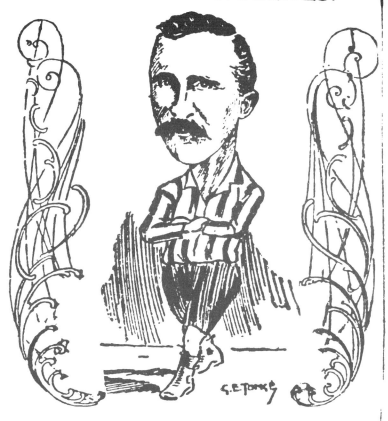

G.E.TORR

THOMAS HYNDS
(MANCHESTER CITY).

THOMAS HYNDS, the Manchester City centre half-back, is a native of Hartford, a colliery district near Kilmarnock. After winning a name for himself in junior football, Hynds came under the notice of the famous Celtic organisation, for which he operated with success for four seasons. A few years ago he assisted Bolton Wanderers during a critical period in their history, and so well did he acquit himself while with the Barnden Park club that they were extremely desirous of retaining him. To this the Celtic would not agree, and so Hynds returned North. However, in September, 1901, he was persuaded to tarow in his lot with Manchester City, the first match he played in for his present employers being against Notts County at Trent Bridge in that year. Since that time Hynds has retained his form in a remarkable degree, in proof of which it may be stated that he has never once been left off the team through lack of ability. He possesses a Scottish League cap, having represented that body against the Irish League in 190?. A fairer or more gentlemanly player it would be difficult to find. Height, 5ft. 10in.; weight, 12st. 7lb.

Above: Herbert Burgess, "The Mighty Atom" at 5ft 4½ins is the smallest full-back ever to play for England. He made 4 International appearances playing against Wales, Ireland and Scotland in 1904 and against Scotland in 1905-06. Burgess also represented the Football League.

PICTURE POSTCARDS.

We are reproducing the above portrait in the form of a Picture Postcard, ten of which we shall be pleased to forward to any of our readers who will cut out the accompanying coupon, and forward same, along with a penny stamp, to this office.

"THE UMPIRE"
PICTURE POSTCARD COUPON

T. HYNDS.

December 27, 1903.

Thomas Hynds made his debut for City on 5th October 1901 against Notts County at Trent Bridge. He stayed with City for 5 years until his suspension in 1906. He was transferred to Woolwich Arsenal in December 1906.

"UMPIRE" FAVOURITES.

FRED BOOTH
(MANCHESTER CITY).

FRED BOOTH, the Manchester City outside left, has, with an ordinary amount of luck, a successful career before him. A hatter by trade, he only concluded his apprenticeship last year, and though the present season is the first in which he has really had any experience of first-class football, he has proved himself to be an opponent capable of holding his own with most of the backs he has so far encountered. Though his somewhat lengthy frame is as yet but sparsely covered with adipose tissue, he has the heart of a lion, and methinks, writes "Para Avis," that many backs have been a trifle sore after ninety minutes' work against the Hyde youth. It was while playing with the club attached to the Cheshire hatting town that Booth first came to be talked about, and after assisting Stockport County occasionally, he was, at the beginning of the season of 1902, engaged by Manchester City. The first match he played in for his new club was against the Celtic, at Hyde-read, at the very beginning of last term, and his début may be said to have been an unfortunate as well as a fortunate one, paradoxical as this may seem. The game had not been long in progress when he and Watson, the right back of the famous Glasgow team, accidentally collided, and both retired—the visiting player for the rest of the game, and Booth for a quarter of an hour or thereabouts. That the injury he received did not effect his play, however, was proved in the light of subsequent events, for his work on the extreme left was undoubtedly one of the features of the contest. Moreover, he scored the only goal of the match, and, indeed, a very fine one it was. Booth has, however, been somewhat unfortunate in sustaining injuries. This has accounted for his lengthy absences from the team, and on these occasions Threlfall has filled the breach, though last year the latter was probably regarded as the regular member of the senior eleven. Our photograph is by F. Chambers, Manchester.

Fred Booth and 'Sandy' Turnbull both scored in the second round game against Woolwich Arsenal.

HAS CITY DONE IT?

PICTURE POSTCARDS.

We are reproducing the above portrait in the form of a Picture Postcard, ten of which we shall be pleased to forward to any of our readers who will cut out the accompanying coupon, and forward same, along with a penny stamp, to this office.

City (Billy Meredith) leapfrogs over the Gunners—City's successful Cup run began at Hyde Road with a 3-2 victory over Sunderland. City then beat Woolwich Arsenal 2-0 in the Second Round.

THIRD ROUND

Following City's 5th round no score draw with Middlesbrough at Hyde Road they travelled up to Middlesbrough for the replay and won 3-1. The Club then drew Sheffield Wednesday in the Semi-Final. City beat Wednesday 3-1 at Goodison Park, the attendance was 33,000.

1904 CUP FINAL

Covered Stand DD,   Uncovered Stand DD,

CRYSTAL PALACE.   **5/-**

The Football Association Challenge Cup.

FINAL TIE,

Saturday, April 23rd, 1904.
Kick Off at 3.30 p.m.

The Holder of this Ticket is requested to occupy the Seat by 3.15 p.m.

No. **989** *This Ticket does NOT admit to the Palace.*

A 1904 Cup Final ticket. Original cost 5 shillings, now a much sought-after collectors piece.

Left: Manchester City gave their name to many adverts in the early years of this century.

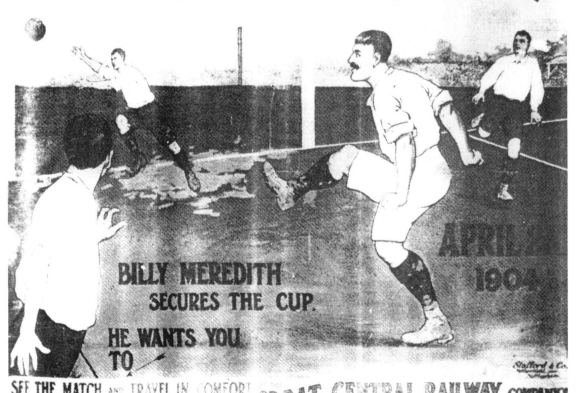

This 'famous' advertisement correctly predicted the result of the game, the scorer, and even the correct goals used. The advertisement appeared outside Manchester's London Road Station (now Piccadilly) prior to the all Lancashire Final.

TWO RED ROSES

FIGHT THE FINAL BATTLE

FOR

THE ENGLISH CUP.

PORTRAITS OF THE TEAMS.

J. HILLMAN.	J. M'MAHON.	H. BURGESS.	S. FROST.
T. HYNDS.	S. B. ASHWORTH.	W. MEREDITH.	G. LIVINGSTONE.
W. GILLESPIE.	A. TURNBULL.	F. BOOTH.	

BOLTON WANDERERS.

	D. DAVIES.		
W. BROWN.	R. STRUTHERS.	A. FREEBAIRN.	S. MARSH.
S. GREENHALGH. R. CLIFFORD.		D. STOKES.	
W. YENSON.	W. WHITE.	R. TAYLOR.	

SPECIALLY PHOTOGRAPHED FOR "THE UMPIRE."

MANCHESTER CITY v. BOLTON WANDERERS

Meredith wins the toss.

Right: Meredith attacks the Bolton goal during the F.A. Cup Final on 23rd April 1904.

A corner kick in the Cup Final between Manchester City and Bolton Wanderers, at Crystal Palace.

MANCHESTER CITY 1 BOLTON WANDERERS 0

The 1903-04 season saw City finally emerge as a major football club. Before 1904 City had had little success. The team had won the Manchester Cup in 1891 and 1892, reached the Lancashire Junior Cup Final, and won the Healey Charity Cup on three occasions, but these successes did little to enhance the Club's national reputation after the Club became founder members of Division Two. In the League City reached the promotion Test Matches in 1896 but failed to gain promotion after losing 6-1 to West Bromwich Albion and 8-0 to Small Heath. City finally became Champions of the Second Division in 1899 and, along with local rivals Glossop Northend, became the first club to gain automatic promotion to the First Division.

City's first season in Division One was successful with the team finishing in 7th position out of 18 clubs, winning 13 games and drawing 8. The 1901-02 season saw City relegated, but the Club came straight back up as Champions in the following season, and then in 1903-04 City won the Cup and finished the season in second place, 3 points behind ''The Wednesday''. Manchester City had finally arrived.

[Sent prepaid to any address fo
3s. 3d. half-yearly:

MANCHESTER CITY SECURE THE CUP.

Trotters supporters.

Meredith puts through the cup-winner.

Taylor makes good use of White's clever pass.

Brown disturbs the City attack.

The Premier greets "W.G."

Hillman collars the ball at the finish.

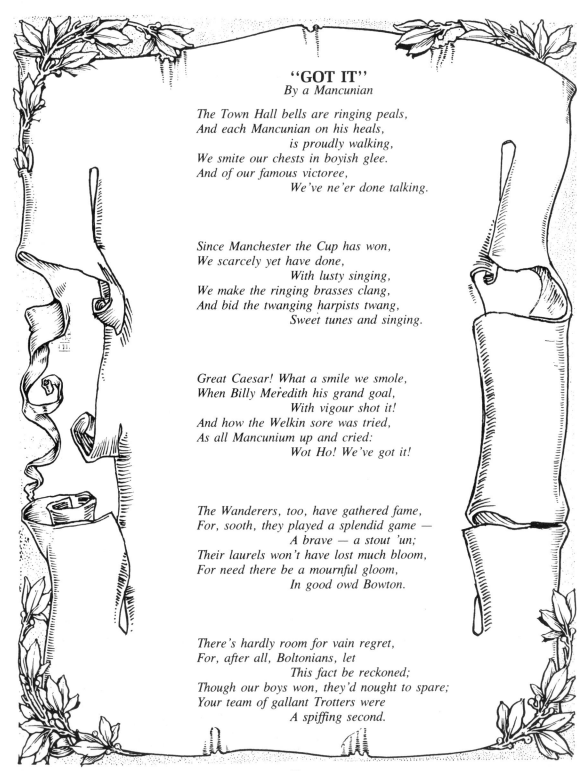

"GOT IT"
By a Mancunian

The Town Hall bells are ringing peals,
And each Mancunian on his heals,
      is proudly walking,
We smite our chests in boyish glee.
And of our famous victoree,
      We've ne'er done talking.

Since Manchester the Cup has won,
We scarcely yet have done,
      With lusty singing,
We make the ringing brasses clang,
And bid the twanging harpists twang,
      Sweet tunes and singing.

Great Caesar! What a smile we smole,
When Billy Meredith his grand goal,
      With vigour shot it!
And how the Welkin sore was tried,
As all Mancunium up and cried:
      Wot Ho! We've got it!

The Wanderers, too, have gathered fame,
For, sooth, they played a splendid game —
      A brave — a stout 'un;
Their laurels won't have lost much bloom,
For need there be a mournful gloom,
      In good owd Bowton.

There's hardly room for vain regret,
For, after all, Boltonians, let
      This fact be reckoned;
Though our boys won, they'd nought to spare;
Your team of gallant Trotters were
      A spiffing second.

"UMPIRE" FAVOURITES.

MR. JOHN EDWARD CHAPMAN.

HERETOFORE "UMPIRE Favourites" have been confined exclusively to men playing the game, but in departing from our usual custom to-day we do so with the object of paying some slight tribute to Mr. John Edward Chapman, a gentleman who may fairly lay claim to being one of the founders of Manchester City; and seeing that this notice synchronises with the club's achievement at the Palace of winning the English Cup, the occasion may not be considered to be inopportune. When, in 1894, Mr. Joshua Parlby—the best of good fellows—was endeavouring to institute a club in place of the defunct Ardwick organisation, Mr. Chapman was one of the first men he approached, and the assistance asked for was not sought in vain. The nucleus of a club having been formed, Mr. Chapman was elected chairman, and at a meeting of the League, on the day on which the late Queen visited Cottonopolis for the purpose of opening the Ship Canal, Manchester City were, thanks in some measure to the oratorical powers of Mr. Parlby, who became the first secretary, admitted to the Second Division. Ever since that time Mr. Chapman has been a member of the board, and for eight unbroken years he was the chairman. The name of John Chapman, as he is familiarly called, is known to most of the many thousands who claim to be numbered among the supporters of Manchester City, but it may safely be said that comparatively few are aware to what extent they are indebted to the gentleman who for so long presided over the destinies of the club. Though now a prosperous organisation, Manchester City has not always been in that happy position, and in the early years of its existence, when an effort was being made to get together a team worthy of representing a city like Manchester—a costly business,—the subject of this sketch was always ready to furnish the sinews of war whenever necessary. In this and in other ways, such, for instance, as visiting different places for the purpose of watching men who had been "spotted" as likely to prove of service to the club, Mr. Chapman has always been ready to render assistance. Photo by J. T. Wilkinson, 43, Market-street, Manchester.

Right: Manchester City's Cup winning team. Standing, left to right: Broad (Trainer), Frost, Davidson, Hillman, Orr, Hynds, McOustra, Mr. T. Maley (Secretary).
Seated: Miller, Gillespie, Meredith, Drummond, Threlfall.

1904-05 THIRD IN THE FIRST DIVISION

MONDAY, DECEMBER 19, 1904.

DERBY COUNTY'S DEFEAT.

The collision which resulted in Paton's retirement.

Gillespie opens the scoring for Manchester City.

Maskrey upset by a shot from Turnbull.

Mercer in search of an opening.

Turnbull heads through number Two.

CITY v. DERBY. Attendance 22,000. 17th December 1904, City won 6-0 with goals from Turnbull (four) and Gillespie (two).

Right: Manchester City 1905. Back row, left to right: Broad (Trainer), McMahon, Moffat, Mr. Forrest, Hillman, Mr. Davies, Pearson, Booth, Mr. Maley (Secretary).
Front row: Turnbull, Burgess, Jones, Meredith, Frost, Hynds.

Cartoon from the "Athletic News", illustrating the match between Bury and Manchester City, played on 23rd September 1905. City won 4-2, with goals scored by Thornley (2), Livingstone, Dorsett.

Cartoon from the "Athletic News", illustrating the match between the Football League and the Irish League, played at Hyde Road on 14th October 1905. The Football league won 4-0.

1905. 17 PLAYERS SUSPENDED. CLUB FINED

City's final game of the 1904-05 season at Aston Villa ended in disaster for City. The game was important as City needed to win to finish the season League champions. The game was played at a furious pace with fights repeatedly breaking out — Sandy Turnbull was accused of striking Villa player Alec Leake in the mouth. Villa eventually finished the game 3-2 winners. Following the game investigations into the circumstances were not completed until August when it was announced that Billy Meredith had attempted to give Alec Leake a £10 bribe to enable City to win the game. Meredith constantly denied this but eventually he was suspended along with 16 other players, 2 Directors, former Chairman W. Forrest and Manager Tom Maley were banned from football sine die. The club was also fined £250.

Alec Leake, Aston Villa player who Meredith was alleged to have attempted to bribe.

Right: Cartoon from the "Athletic News", illustrating the match between City and Bolton Wanderers on 25th November 1905. City won 3-1, with goals by Thornley, Jones and Booth.

37

1906-07 LIFE WITHOUT MEREDITH

MONDAY, OCTOBER 22. 1906.

Aston Villa lose at Manchester.

Coosh scooped out in time.

Spencer inspired steadiness into the play.

Thornley scores.

Eadie's height proved a valuable asset.

Walters failed with only Hall to beat.

Hampton brought pressure to bear on Hall

City finally get their revenge on Villa for the suspension of Meredith by beating them 4-2 at Hyde Road on 20th October 1906. The scorers were Thornley (2), Stewart and Conlin.

Right: Action in the City v. Newcastle match in October 1906 at St. James's Park. Newcastle goalkeeper, Jimmy Lawrence (far right) and full back, Andy McCombie stand poised as City forward Billy Lot Jones attacks their goal.

MANCHESTER CITY 3 MANCHESTER UNITED 0

40,000 watched City beat United at Hyde Road on 1st December 1906. A cartoon from the "Athletic News" illustrates the match.

Below: Manchester City 1907-08. The squad that finished third in the League. Back row, left to right: R. Chatt (Trainer), Buchan, Bannister, Smith, H.A. Gilgryst (Referee). Third row: S. Anderson, Jackson, Norgrove, Kelso, Blair, Eadie, Davis, W. Iles (Assistant Trainer). Second row: Mr. J. Royle, Banks, Grieve, Eyres, Jones, Ross, Conlin, Callaghan. Front row: Stewart, Dorsett, Thornley, Wood, Steel.

MONDAY, DECEMBER 3, 1906.

Manchester City's Victory.

A centre by Wall off Hill's head.

Bonthron scored for his opponents.

Charlie Roberts was the mainstay of United.

Eadie was here, there, and everywhere

Jones converted a centre from Thornley.

Smith, the new idol at Ardwick.

RELEGATION AND PROMOTION

Kelso curbed Millers speed.

One of City's goal chances.

Eadie headed clear from under Newton.

A cartoon from "Athletic News", illustrating the game between Oldham and City on 13th November 1909. City suffered a minor upset in their challenge for promotion, when they were beaten 1-0 by local rivals Oldham Athletic.

Hodson was too heavy for Conlin.

Cook scored from a penalty at the second attempt.

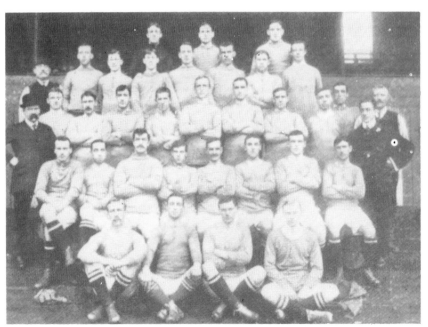

The Manchester City team of 1908-09, which finished 19th and was finally relegated to the Second Division, despite some exceptionally good results: 6-1 v. Bury, 5-1 v. Bristol City, 4-0 v. Sheffield Wednesday, 4-0 v. Everton, 4-0 v. Liverpool. The team was: Back row, from left to right: R. Grieve, J. Blair, W. Smith. Fourth row: W. Iles (Assistant Trainer), F. Davies, A. Winterburn, W. Bottomley, J. Wilkinson, D. Coupe, E. Henderson, R. Harrison. Third row: F. Norgrove, G. Dorsett, B. Jackson, J. Buchan, W. Eadie, T. Kelso, C. Webb, H. Hancock, Bannister, R. Chatt (Trainer). Second row: Mr. H.J. Newbould (Secretary), J. Wood, G. Stewart, E. Bromfield, W. Jones, T. Holford, D. Ross, C. Burgess, J. Conlin, F. McCartan (Assistant Secretary). Front row: F. Buckley, A. Powell, I. Thornley, P. Hill.

Cook made it hot for the City forwards at Oldham.

AN AS(S)TONISHING MISHAP.

Oldham Athletic upset Manchester City's apple-cart at Oldham last Saturday.

13th November, 1909.
ATHLETIC V MANCHESTER CITY

Lyall again kept a splendid goal for Manchester City against Oldham
Our photo shows him dealing with a nasty shot.

FLIGHT FOR PROMOTION PRIZE...

The Manchester City airship, steered by Lot Jones, was the first to accomplish the flight into the First Division. Was much speculation to-day whether Derby County, Oldham Athletic, or Hull City will secure the remains.

1909-10 PROMOTED AS CHAMPIONS AGAIN

MANCHESTER CITY v ATHLETIC, March 19th 1910
A Benefit match for the City captain Irvine Thornley attracted over 40,000 spectators

Above: The playing squad for the 1909-10 season in which City were champions of Division Two.
Back row, left to right: Brown, Lockhead, Davies, Jackson, Smith, Norgrove, Hughes, Buchan.
Middle row: H.J. Newbould (Secretary Manager), Iles, James, Coupe, Burgess, Eadie, Kelso, Bannister, Gould, Wynn, Chatt.
Front row: Ramsey, Stewart, Chapelow, Thornley, Farr, Ross, Dorsett, Conlin.
In front: Jones, Wilkinson, Holford.

42

Cutting from the "Athletic News" 5th September 1910, showing the new stand at Hyde Road. City had spent £3,000 covering the three uncovered sides of the ground to provide shelter for 35,000 spectators.

J. Montgomery (Notts County) shaking hands with the referee, Mr. Kirkham, next to S. Lyall, the City goalkeeper. City lost 1-0 at Hyde Road, on 10th September, 1910.

INTERESTING FACTS

E.P. Hendren who played for City between March 1908 and October 1909 played cricket for Middlesex and England. He played in 51 Tests and also played football for England in the 1920 Victory International against Wales.

★ ★ ★ ★ ★ ★ ★ ★ ★ ★

In 1909 T. Holford scored hat-tricks in 3 out of 4 games for City — Bradford City 9th January 1909, Tottenham (F.A. Cup) 16th January 1909, and 30th January 1909 Everton. The game he failed to score in was against United on 23rd January 1909.

43

THE BITTER CRY OF CHRISTMAS.

Manchester City, Bristol City, Woolwich Arsenal:—"If YOU please, we want some more"

1912-13 UNBEATEN START TO THE SEASON

Manchester's New Wonder.

The enviable position occupied by Manchester City is unquestionably the most phenomenal event in these four remarkable revivals. Manchester City stand out boldly as the only first-class team in the two divisions of The League, the Southern and the Scottish Leagues, with the highest possible points to their credit. The Citizens of Manchester have earned every point in September. Other clubs have remained undefeated, but they have not annexed the maximum marks.

Nine years have passed since Manchester City commenced a campaign in this stimulating style. In September of 1911 they obtained three points in three drawn games, in 1910 three points, in 1909 five points, in 1908 four points, in 1907 six points, in 1906 four points, in 1905 nine points out of a possible twelve, in 1904 four points, and in 1903 eight points, or the highest possible.

To contrast these two opening months in which every match has been won is interesting. Thus :—

1903.		1912.	
Sept. 5. Derby	2—2	Sept. 2. Notts County	1—0
„ 12. *Derby County	3—1	„ 7. *Mid United	2—0
„ 19. *Wolverh'ton	6—1	„ 14. *Aston Villa	1—0
„ 26. *Notts County	3—0	„ 21. Liverpool	2—0
		„ 28. *Bolton Wan	2—0

In 1903 Manchester City defeated four capable Midland clubs by an aggregate of 11—3, but in 1912 they have mastered strong opponents as a body by 7—1, their foes including no fewer than three ex-champions of The League.

Such a transformation in their fortunes after nine years will be very welcome and comforting to supporters whose loyalty has often been tested but has never failed.

Manchester City are probably the only club which can draw huge gates when they are a losing team. Their financial possibilities as a winning team cannot be assessed, as their gate receipts against Aston Villa were £1,009 18s. 3d., representing 32,843 persons, and against Bolton Wanderers' £1,131 1s. 6d. paid by 33,871 spectators.

Manchester City have had a magnificent autumn tonic. In 1903 they lost their first match in October, Sheffield United being their conquerors. Their patrons hope that the coincidence will not be extended in this manner next Saturday against the same club at Bramall-lane.

A report from the "Athletic News" which acknowledges the enormous support City received.

Bill Eadie (City) shakes hands with Billy Meredith (United) prior to the big "Derby" match at Old Trafford. Meredith had signed for United after being suspended from City in 1906. United had decided to make this match a benefit for Meredith. The attendance was 38,911 and Wynn scored the only goal which allowed City the victory.

The young Meredith in the shirt of Manchester City.

MANCHESTER CITY AT THE OLDHAM TOLL GATE.

MANCHESTER CITY "What d'yer say? Give yer two points before yer opens the gate?"
THE OLDHAM ATHLETE: "Yes, that's the usual thing here. Of course, sometimes I lets them off with one point when they're hard up or out of luck, but I see yer've been in clover, so I wants the maximum from yer."

Left: Cartoon illustrating the City v. Oldham Athletic match on 19th October 1912 which Oldham won 2-1.

Left: Manchester City give their name to a football boot.

The F.A. Cup match against Sunderland which was abandoned in extra time due to problems with the large crowd of 41,709 at Hyde Road. The replay was played at Sunderland; Sunderland won 2-0.

INTERESTING FACT

F. Howard scored four goals on his debut for City against Liverpool on 18th January 1913. This is a record for a player on his debut with City.

FOOTBALL LEAGUE SUSPENDED 1915-19

The period between 1905 and 1919 was eventful for City. The team won the Manchester Cup in 1907 and 1911, and won the Lancashire Section of the Wartime League in 1916, the Lancashire Subsidiary Tournament (South) in 1916, and the Lancashire Subsidiary Tournament 'C' in 1919, but there was no major success in the League or Cup.

1906 had seen Billy Meredith suspended for nine months following investigations which claimed that Meredith had attempted to bribe an Aston Villa player. A full inquiry eventually suspended 17 players until 1st January 1907. The Secretary, Tom Maley, and Chairman Mr. W. Forrest, were suspended for life. It was surprising that City survived. The Club suffered relegation in 1908-09 but were Second Division Champions the following season. The Club spent the rest of the period prior to the First World War in the First Division, with their best position being 5th place in 1914-15. During the War City, like so many other clubs, relied on guest players. Billy Meredith returned as a guest in 1916 and played for City throughout the War before returning to Manchester United when the War ended. And so City survived the War and then prepared for peacetime.

During World War I the full League programme was suspended and regional competitions were set up. City won both the Lancashire section and the Subsidiary competition.

e.

NO. 2,109. [REGISTERED AS A NEWSPAPER.] MONDAY, FEBRUARY 28, 1916.

THE CHAMPIONS OF THE LANCASHIRE SECTION.

The Manchester City team who accompanied the record victory of the season in their last match with Preston North End. Standing, left to right: T. Broad, W.A. Henry, E. Fletcher, A.J. Goodchild, H.G. Taylor, W. Bottomley, J. Brennan. Seated: A. Barnes, E. Hughes (Captain), Private A. Fairclough, W.L. Jones. Insets: J.E. Cartwright, J. Henderson, A. Fairclough.

FIVE FAMOUS FOOTBALLERS IN KHAKI

Left to right: Corporal K. Campbell (Southport Central), Corporal L. Abrams (Southport Central), Sergeant-Instructor J. Brennan (Manchester City), Private W.L. Jones (Manchester City), Private T. Broad (Manchester City).

VERY NEAR, THAT ONE!

A. J. Goodchild, Manchester City goalkeeper, watching a shot just pass the post at Bolton.
Photo by E. Hulton and Co., Ltd., Manchester.

A Wartime League game against Bolton at Burnden Park, which Bolton won 3-1 on 29th March, 1919. The attendance was 30,000.

FRAILTIES OF FORWARDS.

Manchester City Again Surrender to Bolton Wanderers.

*Bolton Wanderers.3   Manchester City ..1

(BY THE PILGRIM.)

WITHOUT ever approaching the dashing form and collective excellence they displayed at Hyde-road the previous week, Bolton Wanderers delighted the biggest

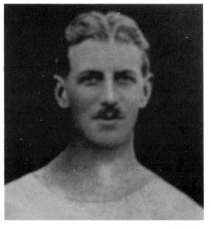

Right: Max Woosnam was not only City's amateur Captain, he was also a successful all round sportsman. He won an Olympic Gold Medal for Tennis at the 1920 Games in Antwerp. He won the Wimbledon doubles championship with R. Lycett in 1921, captained the British Davis Cup team in America, won Cambridge Blues for football, cricket, golf, athletics, real and lawn tennis. Prior to these achievements he had been golf and cricket captain for Winchester College. In 1911 he scored 144 for the public schools against the M.C.C.

FOOTBALL LEAGUE RETURNS 1919

MANCHESTER CITY 1919. Standing, left to right: H.E. Tyler, A. Sorden, A.J. Goodchild, P. Fairclough, W. Newton, T. Johnson. Seated: W. Meredith, H. Barnes, J. Brennan, T. Browell, J. Cartwright. Insets: T. Broad and E. Fletcher.

W. Murphy, outside left, scoring Manchester City's fourth goal in their match against Blackburn, which they eventually won 8-2, on 8th November, 1919.

ROYAL CITIZENS

King George V is being introduced to the City team for the game against Liverpool on 27th March 1920 at Hyde Road.
According to reports at the time the attendance was over 40,000 and the King enjoyed the match. Horace Barnes scored two goals late in the game to give City a 2-1 victory.

On the night of 6th November 1920 the main stand at Hyde Road burnt down. All the Club's records were destroyed in the fire along with the "Club's" mascot "Nell" an Airedale Terrier. The stand was all wooden and had held 4,000 people. The cause of the fire was a cigarette end.

FROM HYDE ROAD TO MAINE ROAD

Following the fire it was decided that the Club had to find a new ground. The Club had often contemplated moving to Belle Vue Pleasure Park where they had already played in the floodlit match of 1889. It was decided that this site was too small and so the Club bought a 16¼ acre site in Moss Side which gave City the chance to build the largest stadium in England, apart from Wembley which had just been completed.

The scoreboard end (present day North Stand) is being built. The photograph was taken from the Kippax Street terracing.

The last game at Hyde Road was a practice match on 18th August 1923. City left straight after, taking a few turnstiles and the goal posts. The remaining stand was sold to Halifax Town for almost £1000. This is how the stand looks at the Shay today.

Below and right: A report of the opening of Manchester City's new ground at Maine Road in the "Manchester Guardian" 27th August 1923.

MANCHESTER CITY'S NEW HOME.

A SYMBOL OF SIZE AND POWER.

THE LATEST THING IN FOOTBALL GROUNDS.

By one o'clock on Saturday the football march to Manchester City's new ground was in full swing. To a cricket match, unless it be a very important one or holds the prospect of an exciting finish, men walk easily and with an air of leisure, but to a football match they march like an army, with a set purpose in their minds and the ferment of the excitement to come already moving them. By one way or another 60,000 of them went to the new ground on Saturday and watched a fast and lively game. This ground is the last word in the provision of comfort and security for (and against) the explosive force of the great crowds that follow the League teams.

There is something almost barbaric in the impression which, when it is full, it makes on the observer. As one comes on it suddenly from Claremont Road, a great rounded embankment towers up in front, and over it at one side looms the highly arched roof of a stand whose dim recesses cannot be discerned at all except from the ground level. Only the fresh green paint on the front of it, picked out with gold, detracts from the broad impression of size and power, giving a rather incongruous air of neatness and modernity.

Looking out from this stand, whose roof is happily so far removed that the air blows freely through, the spectator faces an enormous stretch of terracing which at the highest point has close on 110 tiers of steps; on the flanks it falls gently away to a somewhat lower level behind the goals. With between twenty and thirty thousand people filling this great slope, there is to be seen a continuous sea of faces broken only by two great concrete pits in the centre and two tunnels at the end into which the many-headed monster is to disappear when the game is done. With the crowd actually there, with nothing to be seen but its heads and these pits and the containing wall, also of concrete, which bars it from the field of play, one cannot doubt that it is indeed the monster Hydra for whom the architect has made sumptuous but fearful provision. Come in, he says, come in and take your ease, but here, inside these barriers, you stay, and by these pits and tunnels, quietly and quickly, you depart. This scheme, in its simplicity and great scale, suggests power and force in the way that a pyramid does, or a Babylonian tower, and there could scarcely be a better scheme to represent the passionate concentration of fifty or eighty thousand men

and women on the fortunes of the field below. The grandiose effect is amusingly diminished by the small concrete enclosures which are established at the base of either end of the great slopes. On a sunken seat in each sit two policemen and two first-aid men, their upper halves showing quaintly across the field, like little marionettes or toy-soldiers guarding some prehistoric keep.

Youth in Eclipse.

But it would puzzle the most fanciful to find much of Manchester about the ground. At Old Trafford the follower of "United" stands within sight and sound of the life and energy of the Ship Canal and Trafford Park. The former "City" pitch, like that of Newton Heath in the old days, lay in the heart of industrial Manchester in its darkest form. At Maine Road you may look around and see two spires in the distance, a tower, and a tall chimney, and for the rest the roofs of a few score houses filling the skyline where the great terrace drops away. You might be in Clungerford or Clun except for the internal evidence upon the ground. The grand stand by itself is an elaborate mechanism only to be afforded by the rich town club. For long after the match was over curious crowds explored its many staircases by which the holders of all sorts of tickets are conducted without fail or confusion to their various seats. The topmost section sits aloof and remote at an incredible distance from the field. Like a squall falling suddenly from the hills, its clapping came at times in sudden gusts from far away.

The game was good League football, played on the happiest green turf and fought as hardly and well as though the game had never stopped in April. There were few really young men on either side; but in athletics the day for youth and grace seems to have gone for the time. In cricket and football experience and stamina count for as much, and football runs to weight and "build" and heavy shoulders. There can never have been so many half-bald heads in the two games as there are now, and the veterans hold their own. The only sign of the beginning of the season was that the players were not quite so melodramatic as they will be when the crowd's blood is up, though when a corner is to be taken there seems always to be six captains on one side and half-a-dozen on the other, and the extravagance with which a team throws itself on the colleague who has happened to score a goal would bring a blush to the cheek of the average schoolboy, that admirable standard of reserve.

Manchester City won by two goals to one, and deserved their victory. In the first half Sheffield were the better team, and the passing of their forwards and halves was delightful in its ease and accuracy. The pair Gillespie and Tunstall on the left wing played admirably together. Tunstall combines speed and trickiness with a cool eye for the lie of the field, which is one of the principal secrets of success. In the second half Manchester City woke up, and, after an even interval, were much the more aggressive. They got an excellent goal after a centre from the right wing, and another immediately afterwards when the left wing was allowed to dribble right in to the goal-posts and put the ball across the mouth. But it is idle to pretend that the game mattered much on Saturday, except it was right that so great a crowd, so finely housed, should have so excellent a show to entertain them. May there be many such.　　　W. P. O.

The Lord Mayor of Manchester Councillor W. Cundliffe is introduced to the City team prior to the first game at Maine Road on 25th August 1923. City beat Sheffield United 2-1, with goals from Johnson and Barnes before a crowd of almost 60,000. The ground was designed by local architect, Charles Swain, and he succeeded in his aim to produce a ground to rival Wembley. The stadium's capacity was estimated at 80,000-100,000. The total cost of building came to almost £200,000.

Left: The main stand is almost completed.

MEREDITH IN THE CITY
TEAM AGAIN.

Nearly Thirty Years in First-Class Football.

CUP AND LEAGUE GAMES.

Manchester's Prospects Against Brighton and Hove.

Quite the biggest sensation of the football season so far is the fact that W. Meredith, who has played for Manchester City for almost thirty years, will take his place at outside right in the Cup-tie against Brighton and Hove Albion at Brighton to-morrow.

NOMINALLY the interest in to-morrow's games under the Association code is divided.

In reality, the four matches in the First Division and the eight in the Second Division are of small account compared with the eight ties to be played in the third round of the long drawn out competition for the English Cup.

All the great football centres are directly interested. Three clubs will fight for the honour of the Red Rose of Lancashire—Manchester City, Liverpool, and Burnley—but alas, for their chances of victory only the East Lancashire club can claim the advantage of playing at home. Even so, there is a counter-balancing factor calculated to dishearten Burnley's always vehement supporters. It lies in the fact that the visitors to Turf Moor are Huddersfield, the club that won the trophy in 1922, after knocking Burnley out at the second attempt in the first round. The latter are not now as strong as they were then, and they will be fortunate if they prevent the Yorkshire team from winning at the first attempt.

Not until last evening did the Manchester City directors decide upon the team they would like to put in the field against Brighton and Hove Albion. In the end they have sprung a surprise upon the public, inasmuch as they have elected to rely upon the services of a player who has, literally, grown grey in the service of the club—Meredith, who first appeared in a City jersey as far back as 1894. The famous Welsh international is now in his fiftieth year, yet he is, in the opinion of many good judges of the game, the best outside right the club have at their disposal.

W. Meredith,
Manchester City's veteran outside right.

This may be true. It may also be that the mere fact that the officials have had to fall back upon a player of his age casts a reflection upon the club management.

To all intents and purposes Meredith ceased to be an active member of the first team two seasons ago. Two things have combined to bring him within range of the rather sensational choice now made—sentiment and his own indomitable will to feel his hold on the football stage a little longer.

Though he has not been included in the League team so far this season, he has appeared in Lancashire Cup ties, and, as late as Wednesday week last, with the Central League team. His form has been such that

there has been much to be said in favour of the bold experiment now made.

The chief argument in his favour is that from one of his classic centres any match might be won, just as it was when he scored the goal that served to bring the English Cup to Hyde Road twenty years next month.

A training session for the 1924 F.A. Cup Semi-Final against Newcastle. Left to right: Billy Meredith, Frank Roberts, Tommy Browell, Horace Barnes, Tommy Johnson. Standing behind are Jimmy Broad (Trainer) and Tommy Chorlton (Assistant Trainer).

FIVE-HOUR QUEUES AT MAINE ROAD.

Manchester Sprinkled With Cup-Tie Colours.

WHOLE CITY AGOG.

Football Ousts Wireless and Golf.

NOTHING else really mattered in Manchester, to-day, but the Cup-tie at Maine Road.

Manchester City's meeting with Cardiff in the fourth round transcended in interest every other topic in the streets and in the workshops.

In the clubs, wherever a group was seen in more than usually-animated conversation last night, the subject under discussion was whether the City would be able to beat the Pride of Wales and enter the semi-final.

The same controversialists were at it again hammer and tongs in the train to the city this morning—quite a relief from the eternal golf talk of a few months ago, and the wireless dissertations of more recent days.

FROM PICTURESQUE PLACES.

One Supporter Less for the Welshmen.

Football is beyond question the national game, and the knock-out conditions of the F.A. Cup competition awaken the liveliest interest.

The "evergreens with each ... and very their own..."

STIPENDIARY'S INTEREST

Even a learned stipendiary magistrate who presides in a court not a hundred miles from Manchester was overheard the other day at the air ... if Meredith was playing and how he shaped a fortnight ago.

There was not much evidence in the city early this morning of an invasion of football "fans" from the land of the leek, but the explanation was soon provided at London Road Station.

The first of the trip trains which are to drain the valleys of South Wales of the keenest supporters of Cardiff City was not due at Mayfield Station until 12.40.

It left Cardiff at 6.45 a.m., and was filled with "fathers" from such picturesquely-named places as Llwynpia, Ystrad, Treorchy, Trehafod, Dinas, and Radyr. The fare was 21s. 2d. day return from Cardiff.

EARLY BIRDS

Many Trippers to See Their Favourites.

The visitors who were seen about the principal streets on the way to business were principally men employed on the railways, who travelled by privileged tickets on the ordinary train which leaves Cardiff shortly after midnight.

They did not arrive until about 9.30, a tedious journey with a long wait at Shrewsbury.

There were several saloons on this train. They were asked by a "Manchester Evening News" representative how many Cardiff supporters were likely to make the journey, and they replied that they expected fully a thousand by the trip trains. This statement is supported by the allotment and sale of 600 tickets to the Cardiff City F.C.

But the football enthusiast is not exclusively the man seen about the streets sporting favours, carrying an umbrella, decorated in the club colours, and deafening everybody with a screechow rattle.

GOOD FOR HOTELS

Enquiries at the principal hotels in the city revealed numbers who had come both by train and by road to witness this eventful encounter.

They were to be found at the Midland, the Queen's and the Grand. The last-named is a well-known football house, and quite fifty people booked rooms for the night.

There will be some merry dinner parties after the match if Cardiff triumph.

The Mangas Park club has one supporter who has walked to witness their matches for many seasons, and it was unthinkable that he could be an absentee on such an occasion.

Inquiries were made about him by the "Evening News" representative, who stopped a crowd wearing the red and white rosettes in Mark's street.

"You mean Monks," they said. "Can't" added one. "I don't think you will see him today. He's now walking round the world."

FIVE HOURS' WAIT.

Comforters the Crowd Appreciated.

With all the ardour of "first nighters" at the theatre football zealots among whom were some sporting the Cardiff colours, began to assemble round the entrances to Maine Road as early as ten o'clock this morning.

One lady whose house adjoins the ground, and who stores cycles, said that she had four clients at that hour.

There was really no need to queue up five hours before the match, and those who had put in their early appearance whiled away the tedium of a five hours' wait by themselves playing football.

By 12 o'clock there were literally hundreds awaiting admission.

and contrary to the intention of opening the ground at one o'clock the gates were thrown open before half-past twelve, and the crowd began to pour in.

One had expected to see a very much larger assembly by noon, but there is evidently considerable confidence in the holding capacity of the ground.

TESTING THE GROUND.

It is not yet known how many exactly it will accommodate, but it was generally expected that it would be put to the supreme test by this afternoon's game.

The immediate vicinity of the Maine Road enclosure almost resembled an Eastern bazaar.

There were:
- Date sellers,
- Coughdrop sellers, and
- Purveyors of button-hole cups and favours,

all of whom anticipated a roaring business. The coughdrop seller had the greatest conceivable worse, because the wind chases the ground was most biting, and even the policemen, who were much in evidence, found the need of some comforter on this kind.

A tour round the ground at a quarter revealed that all who had been waiting had passed through the turnstiles.

It was evident that intending spectators had no intention of arriving as early as they could.

TRAVELLED ALL NIGHT.

One Cardiff party who had included ladies was in no better position to make the long journey by road in two chars-a-bancs. They left yesterday at noon, and Cardiff all night and arrived in Manchester this morning.

Rivals' Progress.

The contestants in the English Cup competition at Moss Side, to-day, have earned their places in the fourth round by the following means:

Manchester City	Cardiff City
Beat Notts. F. 2-0	Drew Gill'gham 0-0
Drew Halifax T. 2-2	Beat Gill'gham 2-0
Drew Halifax T. 0-0	Beat Arsenal ... 1-0
Beat Halifax T. 3-0	Beat Bristol C'y 3-0
Beat Brighton.. 5-1	

MUDDY ARENA.

Trying Conditions for the Cup-tie Teams.

AN inspection of the ground at Moss Side this afternoon, before the City turned out to meet Cardiff City in the fourth round of the Cup Competition, revealed the fact that it was in a shockingly bad condition as might only have been expected after the harsh weather of last week.

It would be an exaggeration to say that the playing pitch was ankle deep in mud, but in places it was almost impossible for anyone not wearing studs to secure a foothold.

Fortunately the surface dried rapidly under the influence of a ripping breeze and sunshine from a cloudless sky.

Nevertheless, sand in pit had been spread across the ground much more plentifully than it had been.

As anticipated, Manchester had to take the field without either Sh... or Murphy, both of whom are on the injured list.

TEAM CHANGES.

Until yesterday the home was entertained that the last named would be able to play, but he failed to pass a severe test and it was wisely determined to run no risk.

As both Daniels and Hicks were also laid aside the expedient of playing Johnson at outside left was resorted to. He had a trial in his position in mid week and so acquitted himself well enough to justify his inclusion to-day.

As for the vacancy on the half-back line, this was filled by W... who played on the left wing. Prince ... going over to the other wing.

These were the only changes compared with the team successful at Brighton.

CARDIFF AT FULL STRENGTH.

Cardiff City had their full team out, so that the opposing sides were as follows:
Manchester City, F. Mitchell; Cookson, Fletcher; Pringle, Hamill, W... ; Meredith, Roberts, Browell, Barnes, Johnson.
Cardiff City ... ; ... Blair, Evans; Wake, Keenor, Hardy; Davies (W.), Gill, Davies (L.), Ferrell, ... ; M.A... Russell, Saunders.

SWAMPED GROUND.

Huge Crowd in its Place Betimes.

Half an hour before the match was timed to begin the ground, at a casual glance, appeared to be well filled, but there were dubious gaps on the huge embankment, and it was not a matter of doubt that the capacity of the enclosure would after all be really tested.

Thanks to the exertions of the police, of whom there was a total force of about 150 or so in and about the scene, room was made for the foolish late comers, and in a little while the concession on the huge embankment became so great that boys were extricated from the mass and rolled over the heads of the spectators in order that they might find sanctuary inside the concrete walls.

Cardiff City followers on their way to to-day's Cup-tie, paying tribute to Salvation Army lasses in Japanese costume, collecting money for the Self Denial Fund.

MEREDITH'S LAST GAME v. NEWCASTLE

Newcastle Captain Frank Hudspeth shakes hands with City Skipper Mick Hamill before the 1924 Semi-Final.

Right: City attack fails when seven Newcastle players guard their goal.

Neil Harris scores his second goal for Newcastle in their 2-0 victory over City on 29th March 1924 at St. Andrews. This was Billy Merediths last game for City and meant that his City career had ended as it had begun with a defeat by Newcastle.

W. MEREDITH IN THIRTY YEARS OF FOOTBALL :
A GREAT RECORD.

IT is amazing, but nevertheless true, that when the furore was caused by the appearance of William Meredith in a Cup-tie for Manchester City last season, he was asked by an ingenuous interviewer whether he had ever played for Wales! Such a question is almost inconceivable to those who move on the great football planet.

The name Meredith is a household word in the game. There was another Meredith, an author; and thereby hangs a tale which shows the fame of the footballer, and the esteem in which he is held. A flaming newspaper placard came out with " Death of Meredith." Quite unconsciously it realised a tremendous sale, for the community was shocked to think of the death of " Billy " Meredith.

So far as he was concerned, it was a gross exaggeration. Meredith was in his jersey as usual on the Saturday, and for many a day afterwards, to the completion, last season, of the most amazing career the game has known. Thus football pays its tribute to-day to a great personality, and a great player, whose qualities have endured far beyond the allotted span of man's physique for the strenuous struggle.

Since the genius of Meredith first scintillated on the wing, mature folk have grown old, and babes unborn have become young men. Football has never known such an epic personal record. Nor can one imagine his like being seen soon again.

What Meredith has done for football in every corner of the country, whether in the service of his native land, that of club, or for the benefit of other clubs and fellow professionals, cannot be repaid on this occasion. But we can at least make the most of the opportunity.

THE PRIDE OF WALES.

One does not propose to go over the whole of Meredith's career. It should be well known, and anyway, to do it full justice would require a formidable tome. However, something must be set down in honour. Be it known therefore that William Meredith was born at Chirk, nigh fifty years ago. To the lasting joy and affection of Wales he missed by only a short distance being England's outside right over a prolonged part of his career, when he was so decidedly in a class by himself that he would have been a fixture even with the English selectors.

Among the latter there have been those to mention regret of the difference in birth. Nevertheless, Meredith has been ever faithful and fervent for the Principality, and Wales for her part will ever cherish him. Fifty-one times Meredith played for country with all his heart and soul. In his heyday recall, Wales was struggling; repeatedly getting the knock down blow, but as surely coming up smiling. It will be understood that during his long association, Meredith did much to advance the standard of Wales in the International arena.

But the same spirit of enthusiasm animated him wherever he played. A football has been a treasure ever since his school days under the mastership of Mr. T. E. Thomas, a present member of the Football Association of Wales, who had a great deal to do with the early shaping of this, the greatest of the many internationals he turned out of Chirk school.

JOY OF THE GAME.

The secret of Meredith's long service is that he has always had a great love for the game, and a stringent self-discipline for the maintenance of his fitness therein. From his infant days when the play of Jack Gordon, the famous Preston North End outside right, made an indelible impression on him, he has always been a keen student in pursuit of the game's arts and crafts. The magnificent result we know.

In the cause of charity Meredith's enthusiasm was never sought in vain. Thus he played 400 matches in this cause, or for the benefits of other players, and scored 90 goals. Moreover he appeared in 84 friendly matches and scored 28 goals. Fifteen goals he scored for Wales; while between 1894 and 1905, he took part in 347 League games for Manchester City, or only three fewer than the number possible.

His club record is astounding, as will be seen from the accompanying details. The only clubs he has had—not for the want of asking—are Manchester City and Manchester United. For the former he played 554 League matches, and for the latter 303; grand total 857. The Cup appearances are respectively 132 and 34. With 236 League goals for the City, and 45 for the United; and 51 and 5 goals in Cup-ties, we have a total of 337 goals under competitive auspices alone.

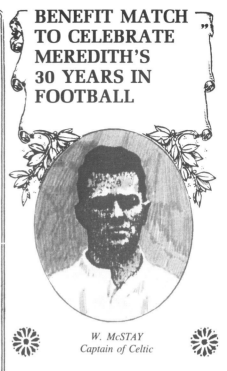

BENEFIT MATCH TO CELEBRATE MEREDITH'S 30 YEARS IN FOOTBALL

W. McSTAY
Captain of Celtic

T. CAIRNS
Captain of Rangers

The following tabulated story tells the tale of what Meredith deserves of his fellows : —

CITY. Season	League matches played	League goals scored	Cup Ties played	Cup Tie goals scored
1894-5	22	16	8	3
1895-6	30	20	10	4
1896-7	30	24	12	4
1897-8	30	20	10	5
1898-9	33	30	15	5
1899-1900	34	18	12	4
1900-1	34	12	8	3
1901-2	33	13	10	9
1902-3	34	24	6	4
1903-4	33	11	14	5
1904-5	34	12	12	3
1915-16	36	6	—	—
1916-17	36	4	—	—
1917-18	36	4	—	—
1918-19	36	9	—	—
1919-20	17	4	—	—
1921-22	30	4	3	1
1922-23	10	1	3	—
1923-24	5	—	5	—
1924-25	1	—	7	1
Total	554	236	132	51

UNITED. Season	League matches played	League goals scored	Cup Ties played	Cup Tie goals scored
1906-7	16	5	2	1
1907-8	37	10	4	—
1908-9	34	10	7	2
1909-10	31	5	1	—
1910-11	35	6	3	—
1911-12	35	3	6	1
1912-13	22	2	5	1
1913-14	34	2	1	—
1914-15	25	—	1	—
1919-20	19	2	2	—
1920-21	14	1	2	—
Total	303	45	34	5
Grand aggregate 857		281	166	56

Left: W. Meredith with some of the trophies collected over 30 years.

OFFICIAL

Souvenir Programme

W. MEREDITH
1894 ——— 1924

BENEFIT MATCH

On the Ground of the Manchester City A.F.C.

MAINE ROAD, Moss Side

WEDNESDAY, April 29th, 1925.

KICK-OFF   -   -   -   6-30 P.M.

PRICE **2d.**

MEREDITH'S XI. v.
RANGERS & CELTIC XI.

W. MEREDITH'S TESTIMONIAL MATCH

On the Ground of the Manchester City A.F.C.

Maine Road, Moss Side, Wednesday, April 29, 1925

MEREDITH'S XI.

(RED AND WHITE).

GRAY
(Oldham A.) Goal

2   3
ROLLO   JONES
(Blackburn R.) Right Back   (Manchester U.) Left Back

4   5   6
BROWN   McBAIN   PRINGLE
(Everton) Right Half   (Everton) Centre Half   (Manchester C.) Left Half

7   8   9   10   11
MEREDITH   KELLY   ROBERTS   BARNES   MEE
(Manchester City)   (Burnley)   (Manchester City)   (Preston N.E.)   (Blackpool)
Outside Right   Inside Right   Centre   Inside Left   Outside Left

KICK OFF   6-30 p.m.

12   13   14   15   16
MORTON   CAIRNS   McGRORY   GALLAGHER   ARCHIBALD
(Rangers)   (Rangers)   (Celtic)   (Celtic)   (Rangers)
Outside Left   Inside Left   Centre   Inside Right   Outside Right

17   18   19
McFARLANE   DIXON   MEIKLEJOHN
(Celtic) Left Half   (Rangers) Centre Half   (Rangers) Right Half

20   21
McCANDLESS   McSTAY (W.)
(Rangers) Left Back   (Celtic) Right Back

22
SHEVLIN
(Celtic) Goal

RANGERS & CELTIC XI.

(BLUE AND WHITE).

Referee - - - - J. MASON (Burslem)
Linesmen - - - J. McMAHON (ex Manchester City)
                    G. WALL (ex Manchester United)

Front and back covers of the match programme for the benefit Match between Merediths XI and the Rangers/Celtic XI.

1926 F.A. CUP SEMI-FINAL WITH UNITED

Browell scores the first goal against Manchester United in City's 3-0 Semi-Final victory at Bramall Lane, on 27th March 1926. Attendance 46,450.

A packed defence cannot save United from another City goal.

1926 F.A. CUP FINALISTS AND RELEGATION

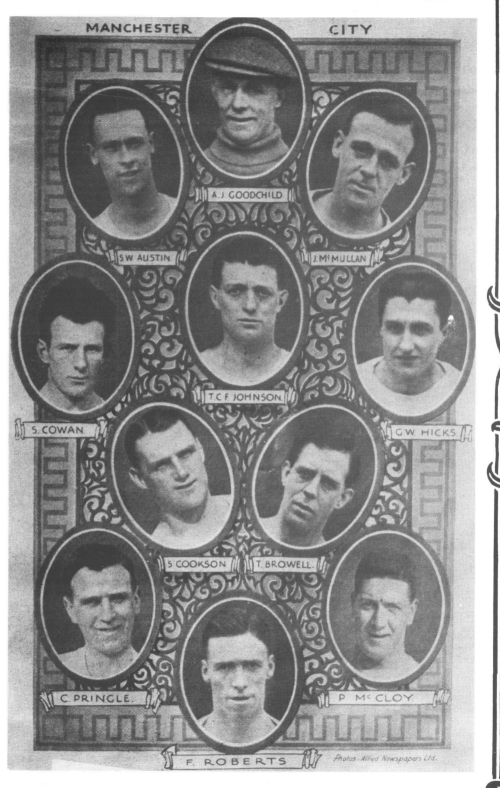

MANCHESTER CITY

A. J. GOODCHILD

S. W. AUSTIN

J. McMULLAN

T. C. F. JOHNSON

S. COWAN

G. W. HICKS

S. COOKSON

T. BROWELL

C. PRINGLE

P. McCLOY

F. ROBERTS

Photos. Allied Newspapers Ltd.

1926 F.A. CUP FINAL: BOLTON 1 MANCHESTER CITY 0

Page 4.
TO
MI
Page 20.

Athletic News

REV
LEAGU

(REGISTERED AS A NEWSPAPER.)   MONDAY, APRIL. 26. 1926.   Postal subscription—British Isles or Abroad 9 9 per quarter. 13/ per year. PAID IN ADVANCE

Cup Final That Impressed The King.

£12,000 WEMBLEY BILL.

BOLTON'S MANY HONOURS AT COSTLY STADIUM GROUND.

IT is generally agreed that there is small chance of another F.A. Cup Final being played at Wembley Stadium, and in that event Bolton Wanderers, by their victory of Saturday over Manchester City, will hold the honour of having opened the ground as winners and closed it three years later with a second victory.

The Bolton Wanderers players—ten of whom reappeared in the triumphant team on Saturday—certainly have made a success of Wembley. There, however, its successes may be said to end. For the enclosure has cost the Football Association—for four Final ties—a sum of roughly £12,000.

When the first Wembley Final was played in 1923, and the ground was invaded, about £5,000 had to be refunded to ticket holders who claimed that they had not secured the privileges for which they had paid. The F.A. bore the burden and asked no portion from the competing clubs. Now the Association has found that, despite its agreement for the Final to be played at the Stadium over a period of years, it has to pay over £7,000 due to the Exhibition authorities on its guarantee.

A sum of £12,000 paid over on account of four Finals places a considerable check on the enthusiasm of those who regard Wembley as the only fitting venue for the Final tie.

Future Finals.

It is the most spacious and ornate enclosure, and it is a thousand pities that this seems inevitable, such a mighty sports arena cannot be saved for the nation. But after all the ticket difficulties that have arisen—and there were further minor scenes outside the ground on Saturday because non-ticket holders could only secure tickets from the speculators at a much enhanced fee - both the Football Association and the football public probably will have come to the conclusion that the Imperial Stadium at Wembley is a costly luxury.

The Stadium comes under the hammer of the Auctioneer during the next few weeks, and it is rather tragic to have to confess that the majority of people interested in Association football will watch its passing, with few regrets.

It is too early, of course, to discuss what will happen regarding future Finals. There are objections to club grounds, which do not provide the festive setting. There are objections to the old Crystal Palace ground, which had the setting but did not provide a good view of the game for all. It was the question of terms that caused the Cup Final to move after the war to Chelsea, but it must not be taken for granted that the deciding game of the years ahead will go to one or other of these enclosures.

Manchester City, however, were unable to seize the opportunity thus presented. Their forwards have scored with reasonable freedom in the season's ties, yet the inside men failed to snatch the chance.

One reason was that Seddon, though not at his best, for the reason that his constructive play was less successful than usual, continually interrupted their attacks. A tall centre half-back can make himself a general nuisance to the other fellows. Seddon did all that, and it was largely because of his ceaseless intervention with head and foot that the City attacks went unrewarded.

David Jack was the inspiring force of the Bolton forwards, who were certainly a more methodical and concerted line than those of the losers,

would have been here easy to extol the winners, but sportsmen who come to see those who lose." His symp out to the losers because very easily have been winne had lost with honour.

The King Greatly Impre

At the winners' banque over by Mr. W. Hamer, the chairman—Mr. A. Kings treasurer, and Mr. F. J. Wall responded to the toast of th Association. In his reply referred to the trouble that again concerning Cup Final said that, whatever had h the past, he offered the assi in the future 5,000 two-shil

The King is presented to McMullan prior to the Cup Final. The gentleman at the back is L.W. Furniss the Club's former Secretary and Honorary President.

THE CUP FINAL THAT IMPRESSED

A Save, A Centre and Bolton Win

A GOAL DECIDES.

STORY OF FINALS SUSTAINED IN FLUCTUATING FIGHT: By IVAN SHARPE.

BOLTON WANDERERS......1   MANCHESTER CITY......0
(At Wembley Stadium.)

THE Cup Final of 1926 was a story of ebb and flow, of periodical turns of supremacy, of the rise and fall of hopes, until at the end of it all the tale was just the same—a goal decides.

I was writing of the trend of the Cup Final, during a dozen years, a week ago and pointing out how in eight of eleven seasons the issue had turned on the only goal of the game and that, quite often, a streaky sort of goal.

There was little new, then, in the second success of Bolton Wanderers in four games. The battle swayed, the goal was missed by a narrow margin, the decisive stroke turned on an unexpected incident of the game. So it will always be while players are human and the electric atmosphere of the Final causes the coolest man to quiver.

This Final was like the rest of recent years because it was all so close and because one felt, for the greater part of the game, that an error—easily excused on such a day—or a mischance rather than sustained superiority, and a score convincingly planned would decide the destination of the season's popular honour.

But it would not be just to Bolton Wanderers to suggest that the deciding point, when the fluctuating fight had run for 78 minutes of the appointed time, was a fortunate affair.

THE ONE GOAL.

It was the result of a flash of brilliant wing play. The ball was driven out to Butler, on Bolton's right wing, and the forward from Atherton darted away along the line with M'Mullan on his heels. The little Scotsman was unable to get to grips. He was never sufficiently close to make the tackle.

But he hung on, and his object clearly was to force his opponent into such a position that he would find it extremely difficult to deliver a centre that would endanger the goal. At the same time, M'Mullan sought to get into a position that would render it imperative that the ball, from Butler's centre, would strike his body and so be kept within the front of goal.

So one construed M'Mullan's intentions. There was little else that he could do. But he failed in his mission.

Butler, crossing the ball from a position near the corner flag, placed the centre perfectly in front of goal—so perfectly and so cleverly that it was really the outside right's goal. As Vizard had had time to close in, the outside left was really in the inside left position when the ball fell astride or so ahead of him —six yards from goal. He sought to meet it, as it fell, though he was not sufficiently near to the ball to turn his shot into more to the ball to turn his shot into a half volley. He did not hit it absolutely truly, and merely forced it forward.

And this Final was like the one goal snatched increases that have gone before, because the ball bounded forward to a friend as distinct from a foe. Just that little bit of luck Bolton had, and Jack put his foot to the ball at point blank range, and forced it through.

IN SIX PARTS.

That is the story of the goal. It came a moment when Bolton were resting after having experienced a rather bad time. In that respect, therefore, it was a little surprising. But it was neither a lucky victory nor a fluky goal. It was a just incident in an up and down game, which characterised in a good many ways, of ...

... the run—until they got to goal. From Vizard's free-kick, Jack saw the ball pass his toe when only a yard from the goal-line; then John Smith and Butler were left with shooting chances—half-chances are welcome on Cup-day—but drove high and wide.

All Bolton it was for fifteen minutes, and the story was the same until half the second of the six periods had run its course, for John Smith, Butler, and Vizard all aimed at goal. These attacks, remember, were generally well controlled. Bolton played to plan, though unable so far to make the plotting pay; Manchester City were a set of stragglers—earnest, but incoherent.

CITY'S REVIVAL.

Part Two, however, closed with a decided change.

As soon as the City began to remember that they had shaken hands with the King and that this was the Cup Final, the fact became apparent to all that there were flaws in the Bolton defence.

The City did not come to cohesion. They did not take up position so intelligently as the forwards of Bolton. But they were abler, by feet, go-ahead methods, in bother the backs a smallish and unimpressive half. Once the Wanderers' goal had two escapes in rapid succession first when the left wing advanced and Roberts called to Johnson for the ball. The pass was sent through truly a forward pass then left the centre forward in a promising position. He moved aside to escape a challenge ...

... their chance. The first half hour of the second half brought no improvement. The snap had departed from the Bolton forwards and, though Seddon was a tireless breaker-up, the defence was decidedly streaky.

This was Manchester City's chance. Could they seize it? For 25 minutes they fought for the decisive goal. Haworth, Greenhalgh, Jennings all wavered. Manchester City sought desperately to deliver the vital blow—a goal would have been sufficient. But it would not come. Hicks shot just over the corner of the goal, Pym had a rare struggle to clear from Hicks' corner-kick, Roberts sent Browell through and, though he overran the ball when the referee's decision in ruling the inside right out of bounds.

And just as Bolton were beginning to fight back, in this match of fluctuations, Pym, in brilliant goal, came to the rescue with a match-winning save. There is no exaggeration. When M'Mullan once again plied Hicks with masterly touch her, were generally well controlled. outside left sustained the high standard of all his previous play by placing the ball precisely in the mouth of goal. Browell's head shot out, and it seemed a score at last.

As it was very obvious by this stage that a goal would settle all, it is abundantly clear that Pym saved his side when he flung himself full length along the goal-line and turned the ball aside. More than once the mighty audience at Wembley expressed its appreciation of individual play—it had a ready eye for the accuracy of sweeping, swerving passes of M'Mullan—but the crowd rose to Pym.

Here ended the fifth act. It was the turning point of the game.

In the closing scene Bolton, reviving again, drew blood—then played with all the joy of boys let loose from school. But how game were Manchester City. Most Finals fizzle out. The City strove to the last kick and came perilously near to forcing an extra half hour. On this the Bolton goal was almost taken by storm on two occasions and, with almost the last kick of the match, Austin passed the ball when a shot might have saved his side.

QUITS!

Not Distinguished But Decisive.

If the Wanderers excel quite for the ...

... often brightened the game. The spasmodic, and it would not to say that they conserved their for the sudden descent or Wanderers' captain often fell in the Joe Smith way, working will from start to finish. Both wings, however, John Smith ball nicely to the wings, and position well for the through pass that helped Bolton, quite advance. But there was little leadership or real reliability in his work.

SEDDON'S VITAL PART.

Still, I counted the forward the better section of the team defence was distinctly sharp caused his friends to quake then made amends by that dive for the ball. But what with the backs? Neither Haworth failing to sustain for pair could easily have been. They were uncertain under pressure that fact must be borne in assessing the work of Pym and backs.

Consequently, I count Seddon the saviours of his side. He finished than usual in his work never really polished, the tall-back was a potent factor in cause his head so often shattered or his long legs so frequently. That was Seddon's part—butting and intervention was all for Roberts, whom he reached, and was a big factor in Manchester City's array of goal finally failed.

Alongside, Nuttall excelled in his half, but Jennings was the resourceful and reliable pivot of recent international days.

M'MULLAN'S PASSES

How much the winners owed is reflected in the failure of City's attack, which was ready of the team. The inside forward achieved consistency; somehow worked the ball well but was not consistent at all. Though he had twice brought a danger to the goal nowadays he did not keep possession of the ball in the game. Consequently, he did not get enough of the ball role in this game was to control the ball and to support ...

No doubt the City was ...

Another City attack ends in Bolton's goalkeeper Pym punching clear.

ATHLETIC NEWS, MONDAY, MAY 9, 1927.

City's Unparalleled Experience in League

A BRILLIANT FAILURE.

Wonderful Football and an Amazing Crop of Goals That Was Just One Short: By THE PILGRIM.

WONDERFUL and tragic. Those are the only words that can adequately describe the thrilling finale at Maine-road. It was a game that will never be forgotten.

I have been watching football for many years, but I can recall nothing to equal it. The atmosphere was electric. There were over 50,000 spectators present, and the one concern was how many goals Manchester City would get. There was never any questioning their ability to win.

EARLY THRILLS.

In less than six minutes the City were one up. From the kick-off they were on their toes, and when BELL improved upon an inspiring piece of play by Roberts, and swung a ball into the goalmouth which Boot caught but failed to hold, the huge assembly was delirious with delight. The cheering was deafening.

Ten minutes later another peal of thunder announced a second success, and as fine a goal as anyone could wish to see. All the time in the sweltering heat the City had been playing football of the finest quality, and at an amazing pace. Their manœuvring was bewildering, and their forwards were as nippy and as virile as they were clever.

Boot had defied them courageously and dexterously when his backs were hopelessly beaten, and shots had missed by the proverbial inches, but when Hicks picked up a pass from Broadhurst and slipped it through to Johnson there was slightest chance for the Brad-iardian. Like a streak of lightning JOHNSON whipped round Russell with a deceptive swerve, and his left foot served him truly.

Two goals to the good in sixteen minutes was a glorious start on such a momentous occasion, and then the crowd had another tonic in the news from Portsmouth that Preston were leading. That put everyone on the best of terms with themselves and served as an additional incentive to the City, who, just as the half hour had been passed, went further ahead with another brilliant goal from Hicks—not a raking slat that bulged the netting, but a coolly and deliberately placed ball from a "take-me-and-get-one pass" by Johnson.

CITY'S AMAZING FOOTBALL.

By this time everyone had been worked into a ferment of excitement—except the City players, whose coolness was as amazing as their skill, their pace, and their determination. And so it continued right to the very last kick.

Throughout the second half they were even more dominating than they had been in the first, and one almost felt sorry for Bradford, who were metaphorically torn to ribbons—all but Boot. Their defence was completely disorganised. All they could do was to kick at random, and except on two occasions their forwards never got a look in.

The City were out for goals, and seven minutes after the restart they had registered a fourth through BROADHURST with as fine a long-range shot as anyone could wish to see. Six minutes later it was five, ROBERTS flicking the ball into the net as it came across from Hicks after Boot had left his charge, and eight minutes after that it was six, JOHNSON whipping a pass from Cowan and again with his faithful left leaving the goalkeeper helpless.

Everyone by now had made certain that the City were "in," but still the crowd clamoured for goals, and the players continued to respond. Boot performed wonders, and Roberts, Broadhurst and Johnson must have marvelled at his skill, but for a seventh time he was beaten from a penalty kick after BROADHURST had been tripped up as he was dashing through, and with the last kick of the match the young centre-forward made the total eight.

Immediately the whistle sounded the huge crowd surged across the playing pitch, and it was only with difficulty and the assistance of the police that the players made their way to the dressing-room. Everyone was eager to congratulate them on the magnificent fight they had made and on "getting back."

Meantime it had become known that Portsmouth had got the lead, but it was not until a quarter of an hour later that the tragedy was unfolded. Despite their brilliant effort the City had not succeeded. The band had played "Auld Lang Syne," but it was not good-bye to the Second Division. By some infinitesimal fraction of a goal they have to go through it all again.

Joy was turned to a disappointment that could be felt, but everyone's sympathy was extended to the players and the club. Never has there been such a cruel blow of fate in the history of the League.

More than once has goal average decided the promotion race, but never has there been a finer fight than this, and never has a club had such a distressing experience as the City. To lose their position in the First Division by their failure to convert a penalty kick in their concluding match one season, and miss promotion by such a slender margin the next, after running up such a score, is without a parallel.

Another goal would have done it, and that there was not another goal, and more than one, was due to Boot. He was fortunate on occasion, but he played like one inspired, and though he was at fault when the first point was recorded, that is the only blemish on a display that, like the game, will, as I have said, never be forgotten.

Manchester City. — Gray; Cookson, M'Cloy; Pringle, Cowan, G.i. M'Mullan; Bell (P.), Roberts, Broadhurst, Johnson, and Hicks.

Bradford City.—Boot; Russell, Watson; Knox, Bancroft, Poole; Hamilton, Patterson, Alcock, Batten, and M'Millan.

Referee: T. G. Bryan, Willenhall.

PROFIT AND LOSS ACCOUNT, Year ended 11th May, 1929.

	£ s. d.	£ s. d.		£ s. d.	£ s.
1929			1928		
May 11 To Balance down		42548 18 5	May 13 By Balance		41377 17 1
			1929		
			May 11 .. Cottage Rents	91 0 0	
			.. Profit as per Revenue A/c.	1080 0 6	1171 0
		£42548 18 5			£42548 18
			1929		
			May 12 By Balance		£42548 18

BALANCE SHEET, 11th May, 1929.

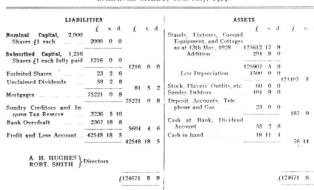

LIABILITIES	£ s. d.	£ s. d.	ASSETS	£ s. d.	£ s.
Nominal Capital, 2,000 Shares £1 each	2000 0 0		Stands, Fixtures, Ground Equipment, and Cottages as at 13th May, 1928	125612 17 9	
Subscribed Capital, 1,216 Shares £1 each fully paid	1216 0 0	1216 0 0	Addition	294 8 0	
Forfeited Shares	23 2 6			125907 5 9	
Unclaimed Dividends	58 2 8	81 5 2	Less Depreciation	1500 0 0	124407 5
Mortgages	75221 0 8	75221 0 8	Stock, Players' Outfits, etc.	60 0 0	
Sundry Creditors and Income Tax Reserve	3236 5 10		Sundry Debtors	104 9 0	
Bank Overdraft	2367 18 8	5604 4 6	Deposit Accounts, Telephone and Gas	23 0 0	187 9
Profit and Loss Account	42548 18 5	42548 18 5	Cash at Bank, Dividend Account	58 2 8	
			Cash in hand	18 11 4	76 14
A. H. HUGHES ROBT. SMITH } Directors					
		£124671 8 9			£124671 8

MANCHESTER CITY 1927-28. Back row, from left to right: Pringle, Bennett, Cookson, Gray, McCloy, A. Bell (Trainer), Broadhurst. Front row: P. Bell, Roberts, McMullen, Johnson, Hicks, Cowan.

MANCHESTER CITY F.C.

Directors:
A. H. HUGHES, *Chairman.*
A. ALEXANDER, J.P.; L. W. FURNISS, Dr. J. B. HOLMES,
W. M. SHAW, R. SMITH, O. SWAIN.
Manager: P. HODGE. *Secretary:* W. WILD. *Registered Office:* MAINE ROAD GROUND.

MANCHESTER CITY
F.C. LTD.

BLUE AND WHITE

OFFICIAL PROGRAMME

Vol. 23. No. 5. SEPTEMBER 22nd, 1928. (Entered at Stationers' Hall) TWOPENCE

CLUB GOSSIP.

OUR WONDERFUL VICTORY AGAINST THE LEAGUE CHAMPIONS.

FROM the commencement of the season, we have asked for patience. We did not expect that our team would be able to settle down right away, but all along we have had confidence in the side and this we think we are entitled to say was thoroughly borne out at Everton a week ago.

The result was sensational, and all the more gratifying in so far as it put our goal record on the right side, but what pleased us most of all was the play of the team. We could not wish for anything better. We were very glad indeed that there were so many of our supporters present, and we have been delighted with the letters of congratulation we have received.

UNSTINTED PRAISE.

We only wish we had the space to publish them, and the eulogistic remarks that were made by the officials of the Everton club; they were very laudatory indeed. Suffice it to say, however, that everyone was immensely impressed and it could not have been otherwise. The chairman of the directors of the Everton club was only too ready to acknowledge that it was a long time since they had been so thoroughly beaten, and not only in the result, but in the play.

It was a great triumph for us and one that was all the more meritorious having regard to the experience we had before the match. As is well known we arrived late and the start was delayed nine minutes, but the fault was not ours. We left in what we considered very good time, but the train did not reach Liverpool according to schedule.

AN ANXIOUS PRELUDE.

From the Central Station this was a most unusual thing. The trains generally leave and arrive to the dot, but it was not so on this occasion, as was stated in the *Athletic News*.

"Travelling by a train which should have allowed them a 55 minutes' margin on reaching Liverpool, they

were nine minutes late leaving Manchester and half an hour behind time at the end of the journey.

"Furthermore, the players, who had made such necessary preparations as they could for stripping in the saloon, were delayed at the ground. The taxis into which they were hurried to Goodison Park could not get through the crowd, and some time was lost through the skip containing the outfit having to be pushed a considerable distance along the approaching road.

"The matter must perforce be reported to the League, who are very strict on the observance of the scheduled time for commencing games."

It is quite possible we shall hear more about the matter, but we have

1933 F.A. CUP FINALISTS

Manchester City team relax at Southport prior to the F.A. Cup Final against Everton. Back row, from left to right: Dale, Toseland, Tilson, Bray, Cowan, Brook, Langford, Marshall. Front row: Busby, McLuckie, Herd, Cann, Barnet, McMullen, Bell.

"RED AND WHITE" TRAIN

City Supporters in Good Form

EVERYTHING was red and white and nobody was blue on the 8.40 special from Manchester to Wembley.

Even the railway company had fallen for the prevailing fashion note, and labels each bearing a letter of the alphabet gummed to the windows of the saloon coaches to guide passengers to their reserved seats were—red and white.

One almost expected the guard to start the train with a red and white flag. There were rosettes by the hundred, the idea evidently being the bigger the rosette the better the cup final.

The trains was so long that its coaches reached far beyond the limits of number three platform at London Road.

The "seats reserved" labels on the coach windows told their own story of desks deserted in Manchester to-day.

MANY PARTIES

There were parties from many well-known city firms, parties organised by doctors, club secretaries, hotel landlords, departmental managers and there were even policemen who had a day off in hand.

The most picturesque figures on the train were a man arrayed in a red and white kimono and his followers all of whom wore grosteque bowler hats.

In the centre of the train was a kitchen car where an army of chefs and stewards was hard at work.

"Eat," said one of the stewards in reply to the *Manchester Evening News* query. "Most of them will order grub,

Full story of the game up to the time of going to press on Back Page.

but no one will eat much, I'm afraid. They're all too excited."

When at last the guard blew his whistle there was a tremendous scramble to get aboard.

On the way down the train stopped at Stockport and Wilmslow where further beribboned contingents of finalists were picked up amid much shouting and excitement.

Even Manchester Town Hall felt the lure of the Cup Final.

The Lord Mayor (Alderman Walker) had gone to Wembley by special invitation and there were significantly empty chairs in other departments.

Corridors told their own story and attendants tactfully whispered to inquirers that many councillors were in London.

Left: Tilson was surprisingly withdrawn from the City team for the Cup Final against Everton. The newspaper also reported on the fact that City's fans all dressed in red and white, as did the team, due to the colour clash with Everton. This was the first time the shirts were numbered. Everton wore 1-11, City wore 12-22.

CITY 0 EVERTON 3

The City squad are in putting practice at Southport prior to the Final against Lancashire rivals Everton.

Below: Sam Cowan and Dixie Dean lead out their teams at Wembley.

Below: The Duke of York is presented to the City players at the 1933 Final.

1933 F.A. Cup Final. Everton's first goal in their 3-0 victory over City. Manchester's goalkeeper, Langford, was forced to drop the ball when he was challenged by Dixie Dean, and Everton's Jimmy Stein ran in to score.

1914-1934

Between 1919 and 1934 the Club enhanced its reputation as one of the country's leading clubs. In 1923 City moved to Maine Road following a fire at the Hyde Road ground almost three years earlier. The newspapers described Maine Road as Manchester's premier stadium and quoted its capacity as 90,000. In the Club's first season at Maine Road a crowd of 76,166 witnessed a Fourth Round Cup Tie with Cardiff City. Billy Meredith had returned to City and almost took the Club to the final of the F.A. Cup when he was almost 50 years old. City eventually reached the Cup Final in 1926 losing 1-0 to Bolton, but were also relegated in the same season. Promotion came in 1928, City again finished Champions of the Division, but the previous season had seen City miss out on promotion by only the narrowest of margins. Portsmouth and City were equal on points but Portsmouth's goal average was slightly better than City's (Portsmouth's was 1.7755 and City's was 1.7705) and so the team from Fratton Park were promoted.

By 1933 City had become a stable First Division side obtaining 3rd position in 1930 behind Sheffield Wednesday and Derby. 1933 saw the side reach the Cup Final after beating Derby County 3-2 at Leeds Road, Huddersfield, in the Semi-Final. City lost the Final to Everton after making an impressive start but the Royal Blues gained control after 20 minutes with goals coming from Dixie Dean, Dunn, and Stein to give Everton a 3-0 victory.

The 1934 F.A. Cup run started on 13th January with City's 3-1 victory over Blackburn at Maine Road before over 54,000 spectators. City's cup matches that year were watched by enormous crowds, in the Fifth Round Sheffield Wednesday's attendance record was set at 72,841 and City's attendance for the Stoke City match (84,569) is a record for any game in England outside of London. Tilson scored two goals in the Final to give City a 2-1 victory over Portsmouth gaining revenge for missing out on promotion in 1927. City were cup winners for the first time since 1904.

City's Gate Record of 84,000

GATE CLOSED
BEFORE START

BIGGEST CROWD EVER IN PROVINCES

The official gate at Maine Road was 84,569.

This is a record for the provinces.

FOR the first time in the history of Maine Road the gates were closed to-day before Manchester City's sixth round Cup-tie with Stoke. The gates were closed 20 minutes before the start of the match.

STOKE SUPPORTERS INVADE MANCHESTER

Thousands of Stoke City supporters arrived in Manchester to-day, and early made their way Road ground for the cup-tie match with Manchester City

This step was taken after consultation with the Chief Constable of Manchester, and it was estimated that there were then 75,000 people inside the ground.

The record crowd for the City ground is 76,166, on the occasion of Cardiff City's visit in the Cup on March 8, 1924—the corresponding round ten years ago.

Easily Exceeded

In the replay with S on the last round they tators, and the recor that these figures app easily exceeded.

1935-1956

In 1937 Manchester City were League Champions for the first time with Peter Doherty scoring 30 goals in 41 games and Eric Brook, one of four ever-present players, scoring 20 goals. City's final home game that season was against Sheffield Wednesday and a crowd of over 50,000 saw an exciting 4-1 victory for the Sky Blues. This gave City the Championship and at the end of the season Sheffield Wednesday, along with Manchester United were relegated. The next season surprisingly saw City relegated and after one season in the Second Division war was declared. The 1939-40 season was abandoned after only three games and regional leagues and competitions were arranged with clubs relying on guest players.

The full League programme returned in 1945-47 and City returned to the First Division at the end of that season as they finished Champions of the Second Division. Manchester United were also playing at Maine Road following the bombing of Old Trafford during the war. United's lowest League crowd was recorded on 5th February 1947 at Maine Road. 7,000 saw the game against Stoke.

The Blues finished in mid-table in 1948 and 1949 and before relegation in 1950. The following season saw City promoted again, finishing second behind Preston, The early fifties were a difficult time for City supporters with the Club struggling to avoid relegation whilst rivals Manchester United were having success in the League but City's fortunes were about to change.

In 1955 City reached the Cup Final, again, this time losing 3-1 to Newcastle. The following year the Blues finished fourth in the League and won the Cup beating Birmingham City 3-1 with goals from Johnstone, Hayes and Dyson. Bert Trautmann, City's German goalkeeper, was injured when he dived at the feet of Birmingham's Murphy. After considerable treatment to his neck Trautmann got up and courageously played on for the remaining quarter of an hour. It was only after the match that the full extent of Trautmann's injury was realised. He had broken his neck and was to be out of action for the next seven months. Consolation came, however, when he was deservingly voted 1956 Footballer of the Year.

1934 RETURN TO WEMBLEY

Left: City fans leaving London Road Station, Manchester for their second final in 2 years.

Below: Club officials and directors arriving at Euston, London.

Below: The City squad and officials leave for Wembley.

CITY WIN THE CUP FOR THE SECOND TIME

Alex Herd is presented to King George V during the presentation of players, before the start of the game with Portsmouth at Wembley.

The F.A. Cup Final, 28th April 1934. Manchester City, wearing the dark shirts, attacking the Portsmouth goal. The small figure in the centre is Tilson, who scored both of City's goals, to the right is Brook. Manchester City won 2-1.

CITY 2 PORTSMOUTH 1

Below: Sam Cowan's winning smile, after being presented with the F.A. Cup by the King.

CITY COME HOME WITH THE CUP

Manchester welcomes home the players and the F.A Cup.

Below: The Lord Mayor of Manchester (Alderman Binks) and the Lady Mayoress greeting Sam Cowan below the steps in Albert Square.

Left: Holding up the Cup, Sam Cowan spoke a few words into the microphone on the Town Hall steps.

THE OTHER CUP. —Swift, the City goalkeeper, handing to his mother the silver cup which was thrown to the City players from a window in Market-street as they passed on their way to the Town Hall. Swift caught and claimed it.

Left: The players and officials are given a civic reception at Manchester Town Hall.

Below: Eric Brook autographing a ball following the victory over Portsmouth.

Right: City staff "show off" the F.A. Cup at Maine Road prior to the game against Wolverhampton Wanderers on 5th May 1934. City won 4-0.

The proud City team with the F.A. Cup.

Below: The legendary Drake scores for Arsenal at Maine Road in the 1-1 draw on 23rd February 1935 before over 77,000 spectators. The City scorer was Brook.

1936-37 LEAGUE CHAMPIONS

Peter Doherty scores City's second goal in the 2-0 victory against Arsenal at Maine Road on 10th April 1937. The other scorer was Toseland. The attendance that day was 76,000. Games between City and the Arsenal in the thirties usually got exceptionally high attendances. During the same season City had played neighbours United before almost 63,000 at Maine Road.

MANCHESTER CITY, CHAMPIONS OF DIVISION ONE, 1936-37. Back row, left to right: T. Chorlton (Trainer), F.R. Jolly (Director), Dr. J.B. Holmes (Director), R. Smith (Chairman), A.E.B. Alexander (Vice-Chairman), W.M. Shaw (Director), H. Wood (Director), W. Wild (Secretary-Manager). Middle row: J. Percival, W. Dale, A. Herd, S. Barkas (Captain), A.F. Tilson, P. Doherty, J. Bray. Front row: E. Toseland, R.S. Marshall, F.V. Swift, E.F. Brook.

CHARITY SHIELD WINNERS RELEGATED

Peter Doherty in action in the 2-2, 3rd round F.A. Cup tie against Millwall at the Den on 8th January 1938. City eventually went on to win the replay at the Den 3-1 with goals from Herd, Heale and Brook. City went out of the cup in the 6th round, being beaten 3-2 by Aston Villa. The attendance that day was 75,500.

The Manchester Liners Ship "The Manchester City" completed in 1937 and so named to celebrate City's League Championship. The Ship was requisitioned by the Admiralty in 1939 and was used as a controlled minelayer base ship. She served in home waters until 1941 when she was transferred to the East Indies. She was returned to Manchester Liners in March 1946.

CITY AT WAR

Left: During the War a number of players found themselves having to take on extra duties. Frank Swift became a wartime traffic policeman. However, Frank got so confused that he ended up walking away and leaving the traffic to sort itself out on his very first day.

Left: Roy Paul is pictured here in his role as a P.T. Instructor in the Royal Marine Commandos. He is third from the left in the back row.

Frank Swift carries Andy Black, City team mate but International opponent, to the touch line for treatment following Black's injury in the England v. Scotland game at Wembley in October 1944.

Below: City's wartime programme for the game against Tranmere Rovers on 4th December 1943. Doherty scored both City's goals in the 2-2 draw whilst Paterson and Glidden scored for Tranmere.

MANCHESTER CITY -2 AWAY 6-0

F. CHAPPELL
Goal

2
CLARK
Right Back

3
BRAY
Left Back
McDONALL

4
WALSH
Right Half-Back

5
EASTWOOD
Centre Half-Back

6
ANDERSON
Left Half-Back

7
KING
Outside Right

8
K. CHISHOLM
Inside Right

9
F. LEECH
Centre
L. BARDSLEY
Left Half-back

10
DOHERTY -2
Inside Left

11
WHEELER
Outside Left

TAYLOR

C. BARCLAY
Outside Left

Linesmen :
J. WARD (Red Flag)
J. SPENCER (Blue Flag)

Referee :
J. WILLIAMS, Bolton.
Kick-off 3 p.m.

KIERAN
Left Back

HUGHES
Centre Half-Back

GLIDDEN -1
Centre

PATERSON -1
Inside Left

8
SPENCER
Inside Right

7
JONES
Outside Right

4
HILL
Right Half-back

2
DENNETT
Right Back

BIRKETT
Goal

TRANMERE ROVERS - 2

ORDER HYDES ALE

ONE PENNY

MANCHESTER CITY F. C. LTD.
OFFICIAL PROGRAMME
BLUE AND WHITE

(Entered at Stationers' Hall.)

Vol. 38. No. 7   SATURDAY, DECEMBER 4th, 1943

JIMMY HEALE IS READY!

CONSIDERING that the Manchester City team has been so unsettled this season, it is very gratifying to see them occupying a good position in the League. The club, owing to war-time conditions, has already called on 33 players for the 14 games of the present campaign. On only one occasion this season have the City been able to play the same team in successive games. These were last October 2 and 9 against Bolton Wanderers and Wrexham respectively.

Still, the City, despite all their difficulties — and they have been as badly hit as any other club—have managed to get a team together week by week, and that is their chief consideration. In the process they have given the younger end every chance of proving themselves, and this policy, though enforced on most occasions, is yielding results. They can point to interesting discoveries. I mention their young goalkeepers, Scales and Chappell; to full-back

Jackson; and to Barclay, Dodd, Bardsley, Leech and Worrall.

Here are eight junior players who have been "graded" long before they would have been in normal times, and it is to the credit of every one of them that they have not let the team down. In fact, I will go so far as to say that certain of them would not disgrace any side in the country, and that is a fine tribute to their abilities.

READY FOR THE CALL

MEANWHILE, perhaps one of the most interesting items of news in the City camp is that Jimmy Heale may be seen in the side very soon. I was only able briefly to mention the possibility in last week's programme, because the information did not reach me until the issue was going to press, but I was delighted to see Heale at the City ground last week.

He is in the Manchester City Police Force, and permission has been given for him to turn out again in the City side, although it will be as an amateur, of course. At the moment certain negotiations are taking place

NEXT
MATCH
HERE

UNITED v. WREXHAM
AT MAINE ROAD   KICK-OFF 3 p.m.
SATURDAY, DECEMBER 11th, 1943

Printed by Withy Grove Press Limited, Manchester 4.

1946 FOOTBALL RETURNS

City are Champions of the Second Division for the first season after the war. Back row, left to right: Sproston, Smith, Black, Caldwell. Front row: Dunkley, McDowall, Swift, Jackson, Rudd, Barnes.

Swift saves for City during the 1-1 draw at Arsenal on 4th October 1948.

An unusual scene at Maine Road, 75,194 people see Huddersfield beat Warrington in the Rugby League Championship play off at Maine Road on 14th May 1949.

82

RUGBY LEAGUE AT MAINE ROAD

Pat Devey (Huddersfield) and C. Mountford (Wigan) lead the teams out for the 1950 Championship play-off.

Below: Huddersfield captain Pat Devey with the Rugby League Championship Cup.

Altogether eleven Championship Play-Off Finals were played at the home of Manchester City.

1938-39 Saturday 13th May 1939
(Salford 8 points, Castleford 6 (Half-time 5-6).
Attendance: 69,504. Receipts: £4,301.
Referee: S. Adams (Hull).

1945-46 Saturday 18th May 1946
Wigan 13 points, Huddersfield 4 (Half-time 5-4).
Attendance: 67,136. Receipts: £8,386.
Referee: A.S. Dobson (Featherstone).

1946-47 Saturday 21st June 1947
Wigan 13 points, Dewsbury 4 (Half-time 0-2).
Attendance: 40,599. Receipts: £5,894.
Referee: A.S. Dobson (Pontefract).

1947-48 Saturday 8th May 1948
Warrington 15 points, Bradford Northern 5
(Half-time 5-0).
Attendance: 69,143. Receipts: £9,791.
Referee: A.S. Dobson (Featherstone).

1948-49 Saturday 14th May 1949
Huddersfield 13 points, Warrington 12
(Half-time 8-0).
Attendance: 75,194. Receipts: £11,073.
Referee: M. Coates (Pudsey).

1949-50 Saturday 13th May 1950
Wigan 20 points, Huddersfield 2 (Half time 10-0).
Attendance: 65,065. Receipts: £11,500.
Referee: M. Coates (Pudsey).

1950-51 Saturday 12th May 1951
Workington Town 26 points, Warrington 11
(Half-time 3-8).
Attendance: 61,618. Receipts: £10,993.
Referee: A. Hill (Dewsbury).

1952-53 Saturday 9th May 1953
St. Helens 24 points, Halifax 14 (Half-time 13-7).
Attendance: 51,083. Receipts: £11,500.
Referee: A. Hill (Dewsbury).

1953-54 Saturday 8th May 1954
Warrington 8 points, Halifax 7
(Half-time 4-7).
Attendance: 36,519. Receipts: £9,076.
Referee: A. Hill (Dewsbury).

1954-55 Saturday 14th May 1955
Warrington 7 points, Oldham 3 (Half-time 3-3).
Attendance: 49,434. Receipts: £11,516.
Referee: A. Hill (Dewsbury).

1955-56 Saturday 12th May 1956
Hull 10 points, Halifax 9 (Half-time 8-0).
Attendance: 36,675. Receipts: £9,179.
Referee: C.F. Appleton (Warrington).

LEAGUE GAMES
1986-87 18th January 1987
Oldham 20 points, Featherstone Rovers 16.
Attendance: 2,719. Referee: G. Berry (Batley).

19th January 1987
Warrington 24 points, Barrow 20.
Attendance: 2.215. Referee: J. McDonald (Wigan).

1949 TRAUTMANN ARRIVES

Above: Bert Trautmann in a prisoner of war team line-up at Ashton-in-Makerfield in 1947. Trautmann was a German paratrooper, who was captured by the British and taken to the P.O.W. camp at Northwich on 9th April 1945. In March 1948 he was moved to Ashton-in-Makerfield where he first began keeping goal. When released he worked on a farm, and played for St. Helens Town. He signed for City in November 1949 and made his debut against Bolton Wanderers on 19th November 1949.

Trautmann was greeted by Eric Westwood, Club Captain, and was told "There's no war in the dressing room; you're as welcome as any other member of staff". Trautmann soon became one of the Club's most loved players and is seen being given a lift by Westwood, Westcott, Rigby, Branagan and Hannaway.

Trautmann stops an awkward shot at Maine Road.

Manchester City team at the start of 1949-50 season. Back row, left to right: J. Fagan, A. Emptage, E. Williams, R. Powell, W. Walsh, G. Smith, J. Rigby. Front row: W. Linacre, J. Munro, E. Westwood, A. Black, R. Clarke.

MANCHESTER CITY
IN FORM

Manchester City played excellent football in defeating Heart of Midlothian 6-3 at Moss Side last night in their first flood-lit match.

City's young centre forward, Sowden, who was playing in his first game of the season, scored three goals. Forward altogether Manchester had the better of their opponents, who, though clever in their midfield work, lacked finish. Hearts, indeed, missed several chances in the first half and though their forwards always fought hard, they never were so precise and controlled as were City's. Hart (2), and Broadis scored City's other goals, to which Hearts replied through a penalty goal by Parker, a somewhat scrappy goal by Wardhaugh, and a lucky one by Cumming.

Above: A report on City's first floodlit game which was against Heart of Midlothian in October 1953. The scorers were: City: Sowden (3), Hart (2) Broadis. Hearts: Farmer, Wardhaugh and Cumming.

Right: Trautmann prevents a goal in the 'Derby' against United at Maine Road on 30th August 1952. City won the game 2-1 with City's goals coming from Broadis and Clarke. The attendance was 56,140.

1954-55 BEST SUPPORTED MANCHESTER TEAM

Left: Maine Road as it looked in the early 1950s.

Bert Trautmann leads City on to the field for the friendly match against a "Wuppertal" Combined XI in West Germany on 19th May 1954. City won 2-0.

Trautmann in action during City's 2-1 victory over Arsenal at Maine Road on 8th September 1954.

Right: Bert Trautmann tries to keep warm as City attack the Luton goal in the F.A. Cup 5th Round 2-0 victory on 19th February 1955.

WEMBLEY 1955: CITY 1 NEWCASTLE UNITED 3

Left: The teams walk onto the pitch for the 1955 Final which Newcastle won 3-1.

Below: The City team is introduced to the Duke of Edinburgh.

Jackie Milburn heads Newcastle's first goal in the second minute.

Right: Action from the Final. The 1955 Final was the first game involving City to be shown on television.

Left: Bert Trautmann makes a miraculous save during the 1955 Final.

Below: A ticket for the Civic Reception at the Town Hall to celebrate the Cup Final.

Bottom: The reverse of the above ticket, with autographs including those of Bert Trautmann, Kenneth Wolstenholme, Roy Little, Roy Clarke, Roy Paul, Joe Hayes, Don Revie, Fionan Fagan, Bill Leivers and Sam Cowan (Ex-player and Manager).

RETURN of the MANCHESTER CITY FOOTBALL CLUB from the F.A. CHALLENGE CUP FINAL.

The Lord Mayor and the Corporation of Manchester request the pleasure of the company of

Mr R. Louth. *and Lady*

in the Town Hall, on Monday, 9th May, 1955.
Reception 6-45 to 7-15 p.m.
Music. *Light Refreshments.*
Ordinary Dress.

Town Hall.
Manchester. 2.

Please observe notes on reverse side of this card.

R.S.V.P.
(card enclosed)

NOTES

6-45 p.m. to
7-15 p.m.

1. The guests will be received by the Lord Mayor and the Lady Mayoress.

2. The Manchester City F.C. Team and Party will, after a tour of the main streets of the City Centre, be welcomed by the Lord Mayor at the main entrance to the Town Hall at approximately 7-30 p.m.

3. Guests are requested to enter the Town Hall by the Princess Street or Lloyd Street entrances.

4. In the event of a draw, necessitating a replay on another date, the arrangements for the Reception on the 9th May must be regarded as cancelled (no other intimation will be given)

5. Guests will only be admitted to the Town Hall on production of this ticket.

F.A. CUP WINNERS 1956

Right: City go on a tour of West Germany following the Cup Final in 1955. Bert Trautmann is seen here exchanging Pennants at Wurtsberg, Frankfurt.

Revie in action during City's 2-2 draw with Aston Villa at Maine Road on 20th August 1955.

Right: Dyson scores in the 2-1 victory over Blackpool in the 3rd Round at Maine Road. Attendance: 42,517.

Above: Hayes scores the only goal of the Fourth Round tie at Southend United.

Above right: Dyson scores City's second goal in the 2-1 victory over Liverpool in the Fifth Round replay at Anfield. Dyson also played cricket for Lancashire scoring nearly 5,000 runs and taking 161 wickets.

Right: Hayes scores the first goal in City's 2-1 victory over Everton at Maine Road in the Sixth Round.

Left: Johnstone scores the only goal of the F.A. Cup Semi-Final v. Tottenham at Villa Park.

Below: Action from the Semi-Final. The attendance was 59,788 and the City team was: Trautmann, Leivers, Little, Barnes, Ewing, Paul, Spurdle, Hayes, Johnstone, Dyson, Clarke.

Trautmann is strengthening his stomach muscles under the command of City's coach Jim McClelland.

Left: F.A. Cup Final Ticket 1956. Manchester City 3, Birmingham City 1.

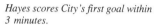

Hayes scores City's first goal within 3 minutes.

Right: Minsey scores for Birmingham to make the score 1-1.

Left: Jack Dyson forces the ball past Gil Merrick for City's second goal.

Right: Joe Hayes in action during the Final.

CITY 3-1 VICTORS

Johnstone scores City's 3rd goal.

Trautmann dives at the feet of Brown.

Trautmann collides with Murphy whilst making another great save. It was later discovered that Trautmann had broken his neck in this collision. He bravely managed to play through the game.

Left: The two goalkeepers Merrick and Trautmann after the game.

1956 F.A. CUP WINNERS AGAIN

The Queen presents the F.A. Cup to Roy Paul, closely watched by Clarke and Barnes.

Right: Roy Paul pictured with his son, Robert, and the F.A. Cup.

Below: Roy Paul holds the Cup whilst being chaired round the stadium by Dave Ewing, Don Revie and Ken Barnes, following the 3-1 victory over Birmingham City.

Above: 1956 Cup Winners. Back row, left to right: A. Douglas, R. Smith, W. Smith, F.R. Jolly, E. Gill. Middle row: L.H. Barnett, K. Barnes, W. Leivers, B. Trautmann, Dave Ewing, R. Little, L. McDowall. Front row: R. Johnstone, J. Hayes, R. Paul, D. Revie, J. Dyson, R. Clarke.

Above: Bert Trautmann and Roy Paul in training. Trautmann's return to League football following his broken neck was Wolverhampton Wanderers' 3-2 victory over City on 15th December 1956. Attendance: 30,329. The match appeared on BBC's "Sports Special" the same night. This was the first time a match had been televised at Maine Road.

Left: Tait scores from the penalty spot during Newcastle's 5-4 victory over City in the 3rd Round F.A. Cup Replay at Maine Road. Attendance: 46,988, on 9th January 1957.

THE LEGENDARY FRANK SWIFT IS KILLED AT MUNICH

MANCHESTER CITY F.C.

SUPPORTERS CLUB (1949)

Inauguration of MR. F. V. SWIFT
Ex-Manchester City / England Goalkeeper
as President of Supporters Club at a

Dinner

&

Social Evening

SATURDAY, 28th SEPTEMBER 1957

at Manchester & Salford Co-op Cafe,
Downing Street,
Manchester, 1.

Frank Swift had only been President of the Supporter's Club for six months when he was tragically killed in the Munich air disaster on 6th February 1958. Swift had followed Manchester United for their European Cup Quarter Final match against Belgrade as a newspaper reporter.

INTERESTING FACTS

Manchester City became the first club to reach the F.A. Cup Final at Wembley in successive seasons, 1933 and 1934 and again in 1955 and 1956.

*   *   *

Bobby Johnstone became the first man to score in successive Wembley Finals (1955 and 1956).

MANCHESTER CITY 1958-59. Back row, left to right: J. McTavish, C. Sear, B. Trautmann, K. Barnes, D. Ewing, W. Leivers. Front row: C. Barlow, W.S. Hayes, R. Johnstone, W. McAdams, R. Sambrook. Inset: G. Hannah.

INTERESTING FACT
Glynn Pardoe became City's youngest player when he made his debut in the game against Birmingham City on 11th April 1962 at Maine Road.

Above: Denis Law scores on his debut for City on 19th March 1960 at Leeds. Leeds United won the game 4-3.

Left: Trautmann dives for the ball as Leivers and Sear look on in horror during Arsenal's 2-1 victory at Highbury on 2nd November 1957. Attendance: 43,664.

The last game of the 1959-60 season saw Burnley win 2-1 to clinch the League Championship in front of 65,981 spectators at Maine Road. This is the first Burnley goal scored by Brian Pilkington (not in picture).

The City squad for the 1963-64 season. City had been relegated the previous season. Despite being in the Second Division City still managed to get to the Semi-Final of the League Cup, going out to Stoke City (2-1) on aggregate.
Back row, left to right: G. Howard, G. Pardoe, R. Cunliffe, S. Goddard, D. Panter, B. Mullin, J. Clay, D. Hodgkinson, R. McAlinden, R. Frost, G. Chadwick, D. Connor, M. Doyle. Middle row: G.H. Poyser (Manager), F. Tilson (Chief Scout), R. Kennedy, C.R. Sear, M. Gray, G. Hannah, P.E. Aimson, H.W. Dowd, D. Wagstaffe, V. Gomersall, D.F. Shawcross, M. Batty, A.H. Wood, L.H. Barnett (Physiotherapist), W. Griffiths (Secretary). Front row: J. Meadows (1st Team Trainer), N.J. Young, J.H. Benson, R.A.J. Cheetham, J.B. Betts, A.A. Oakes, J. Hayes, W.E. Leivers, P.A. Dobing, A. Harley, J.P. Hart (2nd Team Trainer).

JOE MERCER ARRIVES

Right: Joe Mercer gives a press conference on his first day at City, watched by Chairman Albert Alexander and Walter Griffiths (Secretary), in July 1965.

Below: Words from a present day supporter's song "Joe Mercer came, we played the game, we went to Rotherham, we won 1-0 and we went back into Division One . . .".
Colin Bell heads the only goal of the game against Rotherham on 4th May 1966. Attendance: 11,376.

Above: Mike Summerbee scores City's first goal at Carlisle on 26th February 1966. City won the game 2-1 with the other goal coming from Glyn Pardoe.

The City squad with the Second Division Championship Trophy.

Right: Harry Dowd and Glyn Pardoe prevent former City player Peter Dobling from scoring in City's 1-0 victory over Stoke on 12th November 1966.

Left: Maine Road as it looked in the mid-sixties.

1967/68 LEAGUE CHAMPIONS AGAIN

Above: Action during the opening League game of the 1967-68 season against Liverpool. In the picture Colin Bell collides with Alan Ogley watched by David Connor and Glyn Pardoe. A crowd of 49,000 watched this 0-0 draw at Maine Road.

Right: Mike Summerbee scores City's second goal against Coventry on 9th September 1967.

Left: Harry Dowd takes it easy at Coventry.

Below: Paul Hince pushes the ball past Coventry keeper Glazier to Mike Summerbee for him to score City's second goal in the 3-0 victory at Coventry on 9th September 1967. The three scorers were Hince, Bell and Summerbee.

THE CRUSHING OF THE REDS OR
WHEN THE REDS TURN BLUE

27th. Day of March, A Wednesday night
United they did die of fright
Although Best scored in the first minute
After that they were never in it.

Summerbee said to his mate Best
You can sit back now and take a rest
In the 17th minute the Red Wall fell
with a fantastic goal by Colin Bell.

United half time it was a draw
and we didn't see much of the 'Mighty Law'
12 minutes after half time break
A header by Heslop was a piece of cake.

Now City are leading two goals to one
The United fans don't think it's fun
Nobby Stiles was playing Merry Hell
and practically crippled world class Bell.

We saw the end of 'Hot Shot' Herd
to be replaced by another bird
He came on to raise the flag
But he couldn't pop a paper bag.

Burns was getting really rattled
trying to keep Francis Lee shackled
when he had finished, Bell was floored
and from a penalty, Francis Lee scored.

3 goals to 1 at the end of play
Superb skill had won the day
The City slickers were home and dry
leaving the United fans to moan and cry.

Joe and Malcolm reign supreme
as City thrashed the so called 'Cream'
The fans went wild with Jubiliation
as they watched United's Annihilation.

Sir Alf was there to see his red pets
Said "I won't pick any of these red pets
of the City players at my call
for Mexico I will pick them all".

City are Manchester's Pride
and United are on the slide
From Real Madrid came the News
"Thank God, we're not playing the Blues".

Now Busby sits there all forlorn
watching his team all tattered and torn
He wonders what it is all about
Since City snuffed United out.

Poem produced after City defeated United 3-1 at
Old Trafford, on 27th March 1968.
Attendance 63,400.

1957-73

Following City's successes in the mid-fifties the Club spent the rest of the fifties and early sixties fighting to avoid relegation. In March 1960 City paid a then record transfer fee of £55,000 to sign Denis Law from Huddersfield Town, but three years later the inevitable happened. City were relegated. Les McDowall had managed the Club since 1950 but was unable to prevent City's relegation and so George Poyser was promoted from Assistant Manager. Apart from a League Cup Semi-Final appearance the Club continued on a downward spiral. City's average League attendance for the 1964-65 season was just below 15,000 — the lowest since 1898-99. George Poyser resigned before the end of the season. It looked as if Manchester City would never return to the First Division when they appeared to make a bold move by appointing Joe Mercer, former England Captain and Aston Villa Manager, as the new Manager.

Mercer's first season in charge saw City finish as Champions of the Second Division for a record sixth time. The season also saw Colin Bell make his City debut scoring in his first game against Derby on 19th March 1966. The next season saw City finish fifteenth and reach the Sixth Round of the F.A.Cup for the second year running.

The 1967-68 season got off to a bad start with the team drawing with Liverpool on the opening day of the season. City lost the next two games away to Southampton and Stoke before recording the first victory of the season on 30th August beating Southampton 4-2 at Maine Road. City then marched forward winning the next four games before losing 2-0 at Arsenal on 23rd September. The rest of the season became a race for the Championship between City and local rivals United, with City taking the Championship in the last game.

The next two seasons saw City win the Charity Shield, F.A.Cup, League Cup, and European Cup Winners Cup. In 1970 City became the first English Club to win a major English and European Trophy in the same season.

The next couple of seasons saw City finish 11th and then 4th in 1971-72 missing the Championship by a single point. A battle had taken place for control of the Club amongst the Board of Directors. Malcolm Allison had become involved and almost lost his position with the Club. Joe Mercer stood by Allison but eventually, in June 1972, it was Mercer who left the Club. Allison was now in total charge but realised that he could no longer motivate the players and so left before the end of the season.

MAKE WAY FOR MERCER

Manchester City manager Joe Mercer enjoys a cup of tea before leaving for Newcastle yesterday.

FORECASTING the result of the Football League championship that will be decided today is, I am assured by everyone, a simple formality.

Everyone seems happily certain that Joe Mercer's Manchester City will win at Newcastle today and make Manchester United's victory over Sunderland add up to a fraction less than enough . . . that Maine-road will take over the title from Old Trafford.

It has all been worked out with logic, statistics and facts—rather like algebra The theorists make comforting sense when they point out that because the Manchester teams have proved to have not only better players but sounder tactics more impressive records and greater incentives than Newcastle and Sunderland they will win.

The slight snag is that football is not as logical as mathematics nor as leisurely as chess.

Matches are not won by debate or argument but by men—by their mood and by their mistakes. Players are humans—and humans have a habit of confounding computers.

Forty-four very human players, capable of anything from errors they would normally never make to magnificence no one can be certain is beyond them, will decide this championship.

Because of that fact it is far easier to fire questions than supply answers right now.

What right, for instance, has anyone to assume that Sunderland, a team secure in a seam of confidence, cannot get a draw or better at Old Trafford today?

For a start, Alan Brown the Sunderland boss, a man who has never displayed any notable affection for Manchester United, will insist on flat-out effort.

Will Matt Busby's team be as shaky and anxious as they have been in the

By Frank McGhee

immediate past when an important overseas occasion awaited them round the weekend's corner?

Will the lack of tension make both the North-east teams relax to play a free, aggressive game?

Will Newcastle in addition be determined to remove from the minds and memories of their fans the depressing drubbing they took last week?

In any case why should Newcastle, with only one defeat at St. James's Park all season, meekly accept a role as sacrificial lamb for the knife-thrusts of the City attack?

Will the two most important figures in that attack, Colin Bell and Mike Summerbee, be completely fit after a week of treatment for injuries?

Missing

Will the most notable forward in the Newcastle team, Wyn Davies, choose this moment to find the form that has been significantly missing?

There won't be any definite answers until 4.40 p.m. this afternoon—and maybe not then because I hope no one has forgotten that both Manchester teams could still lose and allow the hungry hunters of Liverpool to pounce.

My own view is that the situation is one to which Manchester City are ideally suited.

They have carried .... buccaneers from a bygone age of adventure.

Left: Neil Young is mobbed by team mates after scoring City's third goal in the 4-3 victory over Newcastle, which gave City the Division 1 Championship. Over 20,000 City supporters travelled to Newcastle for this game.

1968/69 INTO EUROPE AND F.A. CUP WINNERS

The 1968 League Champions and Charity Shield winners.

Left: Joe Mercer in triumph as he holds aloft the League Championship Trophy.

City leave for the 2nd leg of the European Cup First Round tie with Fenerbahce. The first game ended goalless. City lost the second game 2-1 Coleman scored for the Blues.

Above: Neil Young scores the first goal in the 2-0 victory over Newcastle in the Fourth Round Replay at Maine Road, on 29th January 1969. Attendance: 60,844.

Right: Everton goalkeeper Gordon West realises his Wembley dream is now over after Booth's late goal gave City victory in the F.A. Cup Semi-Final on the 22nd March 1969.

Above: Celebrations after Tommy Booth's last minute goal against Everton at Villa Park which put City into the F.A. Cup Final for the seventh time. Attendance: 63,025. City then faced Leicester City in the Final winning 1-0.

Neil Young scores the only goal of the game.

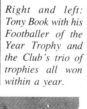

Right and left: Tony Book with his Footballer of the Year Trophy and the Club's trio of trophies all won within a year.

Joe Mercer toasts the F.A. Cup from his bed.

Joe Mercer lifts his hat for the thousands who welcomed the Club home.

An aerial view of Citys homecoming outside Manchester Town Hall.

Mercer and Allison lift the F.A. Cup to City's loyal fans at Maine Road.

Right: Tony Book and The Lord Mayor of Manchester hold the Cup for all to see.

1970 – LEAGUE CUP WINNERS AND E.C.W.C CHAMPIONS

Above: The City Squad, 1970, with the Charity Shield, League Championship Cup and the F.A. Cup. Back row, left to right: George Heslop, Alan Oakes, Mike Doyle, Ken Mulhearn, Tommy Booth, Harry Dowd, Stan Bowles, Arthur Mann, Glyn Pardoe, Tony Coleman. Front row: David Connor, Bobby Owen, Colin Bell, Tony Book, Francis Lee, Mike Summerbee, Neil Young.

Left: Joe Mercer leads out the City team onto Wembley's hallowed turf for the League Cup Final against West Brom on 7th March 1970. The result was a 2-1 victory for City with goals from Doyle and Pardoe.

Below: Glynn Pardoe scores City's second goal in extra time to win the Cup.

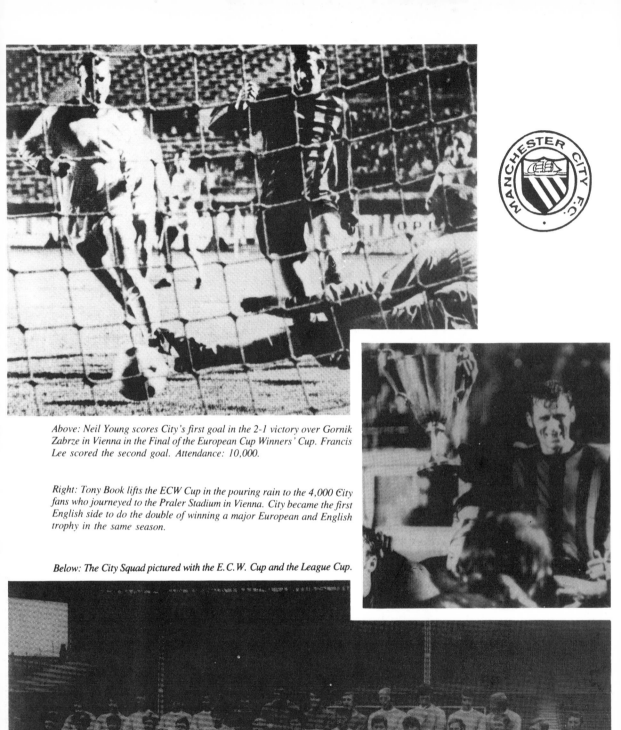

Above: Neil Young scores City's first goal in the 2-1 victory over Gornik Zabrze in Vienna in the Final of the European Cup Winners' Cup. Francis Lee scored the second goal. Attendance: 10,000.

Right: Tony Book lifts the ECW Cup in the pouring rain to the 4,000 City fans who journeyed to the Praler Stadium in Vienna. City became the first English side to do the double of winning a major European and English trophy in the same season.

Below: The City Squad pictured with the E.C.W. Cup and the League Cup.

Left: Tommy Booth is stretchered off during City's 5-4 victory over neighbours Bury, in a pre-season friendly match on 8th August 1970.

Above: The City Squad for the 1971-72 season. Back row, from left to right: P. Blakey (Physiotherapist), W. Donachie, M. Doyle, T. Booth, G. Pardoe, R. Healey, J. Corrigan, G. Heslop, M.A. Towers, A. Oakes, D. Jeffries, M. Allison (Assistant manager)/1st Team Coach). Front row: C. Bell, W. Davies, F. Hill, A.K. Book (Captain), F. Lee, I. Mellor, M. Summerbee, N. Young, D. Connor.

Right: An unusual site. The Maine Road pitch is ploughed up ready for relaying whilst the North Stand is being built, during the 1971 close season.

1972 CHARITY SHIELD WINNERS

Francis Lee scores from the penalty spot.

Below: Mike Summerbee during the Charity Shield match.

Above: Colin Bell in action during City's 1-0 victory over Aston Villa in the Charity Shield match at Villa Park before 34,859 spectators.

Francis Lee scores his second goal in the 3-2 victory at Everton on 11th November 1972.

Right: Dennis Tueart and Mick Horswill sign for City, pictured here with Ron Saunders in March 1974.

Below: Team Squad for 1972-73 season. Back row, left to right: T. Booth, M. Doyle, R. Healey, J. Corrigan, C. Barrett, I. Mellor. Third row: P. Blakey (Physiotherapist), H. Godwin (Chief Scout), W. Davies, C. Bell, D. Jeffries, T. Book, A. Oakes, J. Clarke, F. Carrodus, F. Hill, T. Towers, J. Gannon, G. Pardoe, M. Allison (Team Manager), K. Barnes (Second Team Trainer). Second row: W. Donachie, P. Barnes, M. Brennan, G. Coyne, A. Black, G. Dunlop, S. Potter, H. White, D. Kerr, D. Leman, E. Kavanagh, S. Coulson, J. Hart (Youth Team Manager). First row: F. Lee, M. Summerbee, R. Marsh, J. Madeley, P. Smith, G. McBeth.

1974 LEAGUE CUP FINALISTS

Denis Law and Mike Summerbee after City's 2-1 defeat by Wolves in the League Cup Final. The City scorer was Colin Bell.

Right: Denis Law is congratulated after scoring his last League goal. The goal relegated Manchester United to the Second Division after the match was abandoned in the 82nd minute following a pitch invasion. Denis Law was so upset at sending his old team to the Second Division that he decided to retire from football.

Below: The players leave the field following the 'Derby' game on 27th April 1974. Attendance: 56,966.

1976 LEAGUE CUP WINNERS AGAIN

Dennis Tueart scores City's second goal in the 2-1 victory over Newcastle in the League Cup, 1976.

Drømmen gikk i oppfyllelse på Wembley

«City-fans» fra Fredrikstad fikk oppleve stor finale-fest

Enestående velkomst i Manchester-miljøet

PÅ WEMBLEY: ARNE GLOMDAHL

A Norwegian newspaper gives a full page report on City's victory over Newcastle on 28th February 1976 and follows a Norwegian branch of the City Supporters Club.

Below: The jubilant City team after presentation of the Cup.

Peter Barnes celebrates after scoring City's first goal. Barnes was also named Young Player of the Year that weekend.

Left: Paul Power scores his first senior goal for City in the 18th minute of City's 4-3 victory over Derby County on 10th April 1976 at Maine Road before 42,061 spectators. This was Power's 19th appearance for City.

The City Squad for 1976-77 Season, which eventually finished as League Runners-up to Liverpool, City were one point behind. Back row, left to right: Dave Watson, Joe Royle, Keith MacRae, Joe Corrigan, Tommy Booth, Tony Henry. Middle row: Roy Bailey, Peter Barnes, Glyn Pardoe, Ken Clements, Paul Power, Mike Docherty, Mike Lester, Willie Donachie, Gary Owen, Fred Griffiths (Physiotherapist). Front row: Tony Book (Manager) Ged Keegan, Denis Leman, Brian Kidd, Mike Doyle, Asa Hartford, Colin Bell, Dennis Tueart, Bill Taylor (First Team Coach).

Left: Kenny Clements, Steve Coppell and Dave Watson take to the air in City's 3-1 victory over United at Maine Road on 10th September 1977.

Left: City's first goal in the 3-2 victory over Twente Enschede in the UEFA Cup at Maine Road. The first leg had resulted in a 1-1 draw. City managed to get to the 4th Round following victories over Standard Liège and A.C. Milan. Borussia Mönchengladbach won the 4th Round 4-2 on aggregate.

Right: Colin Bell came on in the 60th minute of the game to a heroes welcome and in the 84th minute he scored City's third goal.

Below: Mike Channon scores his first goal for City on 3rd September 1977 in City's 4-0 victory over Norwich. Attendance 41,269.

Mike Channon catapults himself into the air to score his first goal (against Norwich) for Manchester City.

Brian Kidd is congratulated by Peter Barnes following his 69th minute goal in City's 3-2 victory, which put the club into the 2nd Round of the UEFA Cup.

116

Left: Jimmy Holmes of Spurs tackles Mike Channon during the 1-1 game on 23rd September 1978.

Below: At Maine Road, Prince Fisal of Saudi Arabia lifts the Central League Championship Trophy, which City had won during the 1977-78 season.

Kevin Reeves signs for City watched by Bernard Halford (Secretary), M. Allison (Team Manager) and Tony Book (Manager). This signing cost City £1,250,000 and was City's second £1 million transfer following the signing of Steve Daley in September 1979.

Left: Dave Watson and Paul Futcher in action during the Old Trafford Derby Match on 30th September 1978. United won 1-0.

117

ALLISON LEAVES AGAIN AND JOHN BOND ARRIVES

Dennis Tueart scores his second goal in the 47th minute of the 2-2 draw with Bolton on 29th March 1980 following his re-signing from New York Cosmos on 31st January 1980.

John Bond faces the press following acceptance of the manager's job after Allison and Book had been sacked. Bond proved he was capable of handling the media – Granada Television were already doing a documentary on City which covered Allison and Books sacking and Bonds signing.

Right: Tony Henry scores City's first goal in the 2-0 victory over Manchester United on 11th November 1979 at Maine Road.

1981 F.A. CUP FINALISTS IN THE 100th FINAL

Left: Kevin Reeves scores from the penalty spot against Crystal Palace in the F.A. Cup 3rd Round Tie at Maine Road. City won the game 4-0. In the second round City were 6-0 victors over Norwich.

Above: Tommy Caton, Nicky Reid and Kevin Reeves celebrate getting to Wembley.

Left: Paul Power scores the only goal of the Semi-Final against Ipswich at Villa Park in extra time to send City to Wembley for the 100th F.A. Cup Final.

Below: Referee Keith Hackett tosses the coin to start the 1981 Final.

CITY LOSE 3-2 IN REPLAY

Left: A   dejected Hutchison after his deflection from Glenn Hoddle's shot resulted in a goal for Tottenham and a replay five days later.

Below: Hutchison scores his first goal of the Final to put City one goal in front.

Above: Joe Corrigan and Garth Crooks in action.

Below: Kevin Reeves scores for City from the penalty spot in the replay.

A worrying goalmouth scramble at Old Trafford in the 2-2 draw with Manchester United on 23rd October 1982. At the end of the season City were relegated following Radi Antic's 86th minute goal for Luton Town, which rescued Luton. City had led the Division earlier in the season.

Above: Billy McNeill was appointed Manager during the 1983 close season.
Right: Jamie Hoyland scores his first senior goal in the 6-0 victory over Torquay, in the Milk Cup on 25th October 1983.

City's Youth Team which won the Lancashire Youth Cup in 1983, beating Manchester United in the Final. Back row, from left to right: Steve Redmond, David White, Terry Milligan, George Shepherd, Neil Aldridge, Mike Pennington, Darren Beckford. Front row: Earl Barrett, Andy Mason, Ian Scott, Jamie Hoyland, Paul Simpson, John Beresford.

GOING UP, GOING UP, GOING UP

City 5, Charlton 1.
left: David Phillips shoots the ball past Charlton's keeper, Lee Harmsworth for City's first goal. Attendance: 47,285. Date: 11th May 1985. Scorers: Phillips 2, May, Simpson, Melrose.

Below: David Phillips scores City's fifth goal and his second.

Above: Paul Simpson scores the fourth goal.

This was City's last game of the season. The Blues needed a victory to obtain promotion to the First Division. Both City and Portsmouth were level on points but City's goal difference was far superior and so the citizens of Manchester finally got revenge for the 1927 promotion issue.

FULL MEMBERS CUP WEMBLEY 1986

Above: Billy McNeill leads out the City team and Mascot, Warren Rhodes, in front of 68,000 fans for the first Full Members' Cup Final. Prior to the Final the highest attendance City had played in front of in this competition was 10,180 for the game against Hull at Maine Road.

Right: Paul Power and Colin Peter from Chelsea exchange pennants prior to the first Full Members Cup Final.

Below: A competition that was criticised from the start ended in a thrilling finish, when Chelsea just beat City 5-4 in one of the most exciting finals ever held at Wembley.

F.A. YOUTH CUP WINNERS 1986

Sammy McIlroy scores his league debut goal for City on 17th August 1985 in the 1-1 draw at Coventry.

Right: Steve Redmond lifts the Youth Cup following City's 2-0 victory over Manchester United at Maine Road.

Manchester City 1986. Back row, from left to right: Clive Wilson, Andy May, Gordon Smith, David Phillips, Sammy McIlroy. Middle row: Billy McNeill (Manager), Nicky Reid, Mick McCarthy, Nigel Johnson, Alex Williams, Kenny Clements, Mark Lillis, Roy Bailey (Physiotherapist), Jimmy Frizzell (Assistant Manager). Front row: Neil McNab, Jim Melrose, Paul Simpson, Paul Power, Steve Kinsey, Jim Tolmie, Graham Baker.

SUPERMAC IS SHELL-SHOCKED!

by RICHARD BOTT
Man City 10, Huddersfield T 1

MALCOLM Macdonald has never been short of a glib phrase or an arrogant boast throughout a colourful career in football—until yesterday. This extraordinary score-line rendered Huddersfield's charismatic new manager almost speechless.

"What can I say?" he asked, rhetorically, when he emerged from the debris and despair of the visitors' dressing room. "I'm shell-shocked!

"We started well, had some good chances, gave them too much room for their first goal and then became an utter shambles.

"Where do we go from here? Well, we've got a chance against Leicester on Tuesday, that's where."

It was a day to reach for the record books . . . particularly with THREE players, Tony Adcock, Paul Stewart and David White, scoring hat-tricks.

The last time that happened in League football was in 1962 when Wyn Davies, Ron

10–1 is City's best since 1895

Barnes and Brian Ambler all claimed hat-tricks for Wrexham against Hartlepool.

Nor was it City's biggest League score. They beat Lincoln City 11—3 in the Second Division way back in 1895.

But poor, bewildered bottom-of-the-table Huddersfield have never had a humiliation like it in their history. Their heaviest League defeat was 8—0 at Middlesbrough 37 years ago.

City's youngsters ran amok —and they did it without leading scorer Imre Varadi. Nursing a recurring thigh muscle injury, Varadi could only share some of Malcolm Macdonald's frustration, if for a very different reason.

How the nimble-footed Varadi would have loved a slice of the action. You could have driven a fleet of double-decker buses through Huddersfield's defence and their offside trap wouldn't have caught a mouse with a limp!

Yet it must be said, though of scant consolation to Huddersfield, that City were so lethargic at the back in the first half, better quality finishing would have severely punished them.

The crucial goal was the first, a rare success for Neil McNab, after 12 minutes. From then on Huddersfield were cannon fodder with Adcock—Varadi's stand-in—Stewart and White sharing the spoils.

Revealed

Traditionally, a hat-trick man carries away the match ball as a souvenir. So how was that puzzle to be resolved?

"Tony Adcock can have it because he was the first to complete his hat-trick," revealed City manager Jimmy Frizzell.

"We'll have to give Stewart and White a ball each as well. It's an expensive business at £40 a time!

"For once we gave our fans just what they wanted. They shouted for seven goals, then eight, then nine, then 10. And got them.

"But I feel for Huddersfield. It's easy to gloat when we've had a result like that. It must be terrible for them. We won't be asking them to autograph the three balls!"

Team manager Mel Machin, who remembered playing for Bournemouth when they scored 11 goals in an FA Cup tie against non-League Margate, admitted: "It might have been a different tale if they had scored in that first quarter of an hour."

Even the one goal City conceded came from a familiar boot and, in its own way, contributed to the biggest party they have held down at Maine Road since they went up from the Second Division in 1985.

Former City favourite Andy May stepped forward to beat Eric Nixon from the penalty spot after John Gidman had nudged David Cork in the 88th minute.

Seconds later, White romped away on his own to complete this goal time-table.

Three hat-trick stars

NINE OUT OF TEN . . . that's the goals scored by these Manchester City hat-trick men, Tony Adcock, Paul Stewart and David White

City made the headlines by scoring ten goals against Huddersfield Town in November 1987 at Maine Road, following the Club's return to the Second Division.

McCarthy off

GLASGOW Celtic and former Manchester City defender Mick McCarthy was sent off after being booked twice against Hearts.

for City: McNab (12 mins), Adcock (34, 53 and 67), Stewart (29, 66 and 80), White (40, 84 and 89).

Andy May, well versed in City's changes of mood, said: "We knew they'd be either good or awful. And they were good.

"If we played Rochdale and gave them as much space as that, they'd beat us 10—1"

MAN CITY: Nixon, Gidman, Hinchcliffe, Clements, Lake, Redmond, White, Stewart, Adcock, McNab, Simpson. Subs: Brightwell, Scott.

HUDDERSFIELD: Cox, Brown, Bray, Banks, Webster, Walford, Barham, May, Shearer, Winter, Cork. Subs: McStay, Ward.

Referee: R Hart (Darlington).

Just three of the ten goals. Above: Tony Adcock's second goal, making City 5-0 up. Right: Paul Stewart heads another one in to make it 6-0. Far right: A jubilant David White after scoring one of his goals.

1973-89

The 1973-74 season saw John Hart resign as Manager after only six months due to ill health and Ron Saunders appointed and dismissed within the next five months despite taking the Club to the League Cup Final. Following Saunders dismissal Tony Book was promoted from Assistant to Manager, and managed to bring stability back to the Club. City finished 8th in Book's first season in charge, but success was to follow the next season when City won the League Cup beating Newcastle United 2-1 with goals from Peter Barnes and Dennis Tueart. Tueart's overhead kick was one of the most spectacular goals ever seen at Wembley. The next season saw City's average attendance exceed 40,000 for the first time. The fans was rewarded with an exciting season with the team finishing in second place one point behind the leaders Liverpool. The 1977-78 season was again a successful season — the team finished fourth and the average attendance of almost 42,000, remains the highest in the Club's history. City also had more season ticket holders than any other club.

Following the 1978-79 season which saw the team finish in the lowest position since 1966-67 (fifteenth) Malcolm Allison was brought back to Maine Road. Book became General Manager with Allison now Team Manager. Allison's first season in charge was a disaster. The club spent millions of pounds recruiting average players and believed that a policy of spend, spend, spend would bring back the glory days — it didn't. Results brought City close to relegation, finishing 17th on 37 points. The club was humiliated in the F.A.Cup, losing 1-0 to Halifax. The situation seemed to deteriorate further when the first 12 games of the 1980-81 season failed to bring a single victory. Granada T.V. had began filming a television documentary on City which showed all angles of a football club. The documentary also saw the demise of Allison's City. Allison was dismissed. John Bond was brought in to attempt to prevent relegation. Relegation was prevented but who could have foretold that City would reach the semi-final of the League Cup and be F.A. Cup finalists for the 8th time, in Bond's first season. The T.V. Documentary had shown a revitalised City and Granada T.V. had been given a better story than they could have imagined. City were beaten 3-2 in the Cup Final replay by Keith Burkinshaw's Tottenham Hotspur after being by far the better team in the first game. In the first game Tommy Hutchison had unfortunately deflected Glenn Hoddle's free-kick into his own net to give Tottenham a second chance.

The next season saw Bond sign Trevor Francis — another million pound player. Francis scored two goals in his debut in City's 3-1 victory over Stoke and just before Christmas City briefly headed the table but were soon to struggle. That season City finished tenth. The 1982-83 season saw City struggle further. Bond left after a 4-0 defeat at Brighton in the F.A. Cup. John Benson was appointed Manager but he was unable to prevent relegation and was dismissed following City's 1-0 defeat to Luton on the last day of the season.

Billy McNeill was brought in as Manager with Jimmy Frizzell as his assistant, in an attempt to gain promotion at the first attempt. The first live T.V. Second Division game started on 4th May with City losing 2-0 to Chelsea at Maine Road. The B.B.C. had chosen this game believing that it would decide promotion, however, by that time Chelsea, Newcastle and Sheffield Wednesday were certain of promotion. City eventually finished fourth but had more success the following season when promotion was ensured in the final game — a 5-1 victory over Charlton before over 47,000 fans at Maine Road.

At the start of the 1985/86 season Paul Power predicted that the team would reach Wembley, and they did, but it was in the much criticised Full Members Cup. The Press predicted that the Final would be a disaster with Wembley Stadium empty but they were wrong. The Final was a thrilling 5-4 victory for Chelsea, and the attendance was 68,000 with almost 30,000 supporters travelling from Manchester.

In September 1986 McNeill left to take over Aston Villa. Jimmy Frizzell became the new Manager and although he was unable to prevent relegation he was successful in signing Imre Varadi and Paul Stewart who between them scored 41 League goals during the 1987/88 season. City finished the season in ninth place but the high spots that season included the famous 10-1 victory over Huddersfield, and Quarter-Finalists in both the Littlewoods Cup and F.A.Cup.

The 1988-89 season started disappointingly for City with defeats at Hull, and at home to Oldham. Stewart had been sold to Tottenham for a reported 1.7 million pounds and Varadi was soon to move back to Sheffield Wednesday, but the situation soon improved with City going top on 10th December following a 4-0 victory over Bradford City. As the season progressed the Championship race became more exciting with City and Chelsea taking it in turns to head the table.

1988-89 BANANA BLUES GO TOP

During the 1988-89 season Manchester City fans became famous for carrying giant inflatable bananas, which helped to put the fun back into football and lifted the team's spirits. City went top of the Second Division on 10th December 1988 after beating Bradford City 4-0 at Maine Road and the supporters were top of the League all season.

The following pages show just how much "Bananarama" took hold of the fans and how it hit the headlines.

PEELING OFF . . . A Manchester City fan on his way to join the bunch on the terraces

BEFORE they go bananas, Manchester City would dearly like to know the identity of the fruit-waving fanatic who started it all.

Who, demands City chief Peter Swales, is the originator of Maine Road's BANANARAMA?

It's the season's happiest, daftest cult. The club's latest assessment is that they have in excess of 2,000 carriers of the giant inflatables.

"At first the banana wavers were all in our Kippax stand," says Swales. "Now they're everywhere. They've not yet taken root in the directors' box.

"But there are bananas next door in our executive section. So who knows where it will end?"

It all began when some City fans started to affectionately address attacker Imre Varadi as "Imre Banana" last season.

One day someone brought along a giant banana to illustrate the point and a cult was born.

Laugh

"Now I even get letters from City fans addressed to Imre Banana Varadi says the player. It's a real laugh—and typical of them.

"They were always great to me at Maine Road. And when I played for my present club Sheffield Wednesday in the Guinness Six competition in Manchester this week

Daftest cult...but it's better than bricks and knives

By JOHN BEAN

they were waving bananas at me.

"Frankly, I can see the cult spreading and that will be one of the best things that's happened on the terraces in this country for years."

City secretary Bernard Halford admits police at some opposition grounds have been nervous about the phenomenon.

"So now I phone all club's we're visiting to warn them of the imminent invasion. They're quite a sight," says Halford.

"Returning home from Barnsley earlier this season our fans were held up on the moors. Suddenly drivers travelling in the opposite direction were confronted by a mile long queue of cars all waving giant bananas!"

There has been a commercial spin-off for City. Banana importers Fyffes have taken a ground advert. Banana in-

flatables are top sellers at the club souvenir shop.

"But it isn't only bananas that are trundled on to the ground these days," says general manager Jimmy Frizzell.

"Inflatable Frankenstein monsters, fried eggs, the lot are being waved by our fans. It may be just a hoot. But one thing is certain . . . It's better than people bringing bricks and knives into the place."

Claims

But who is the mysterious creator of the craze? Disc jockey and City fanatic Andy Peebles appealed for information at the Guinness event this week.

And last night, City supporters were claiming that a diehard fan named Frank Newton is the originator. City are still waiting for him to confirm it.

☐ IF you know who's responsible for the Bananarama craze at Maine Road . . . write to John Bean, Daily Express, Great Ancoats Street, Manchester.

E RICHARDS, Worsley. — Surely Manchester City have pointed the way to the whole of the football league. The answer to hooliganism does not lie in identity cards, police dogs, water cannon or TV surveillance but in GOOD HUMOUR.

The "banana brigade" are putting the fun back into football.

If fans have to challenge the opposition then do it by trying to outdo each other in the bizarre fancy dress outfits that are becoming such a Maine Road feature.

■ GOOD idea — but will it spread to the organised mobs?

With acknowledgements to the "Daily Express"

Milner settles in

MANCHESTER City's latest signing has quickly found himself bitten by the Blues' banana bug.

Andrew Milner (pictured right), 21-year-old striker signed for £7,000 from non-league Netherfield — they play in the Cumbrian market town of Kendal — caught up with the fans' cult craze when he posed for pictures at Maine Road earlier this week.

Now Milner is eagerly looking forward to his City debut in the Central League side against Sheffield Wednesday on Tuesday night (6.45 pm).

And he will be joined by two other non-league recruits as City scour the bargain basement for further reinforcements.

With acknowledgements to the "Manchester Evening News".

Banana army take a salute

By Paul Hince

A POLICE chief today paid tribute to the banana-waving fans of Manchester City who helped produce record receipts of £60,100 at Oldham Athletic on Saturday.

An estimated 12,000 City fans boosted the gate at Boundary Park to 19,200 . . . with not one arrest reported.

Chief Superintendent John Halliwell, who helped co-ordinate the police operation at Boundary Park, said: "Nine fans were ejected from the ground but nobody caused sufficient trouble to warrant an arrest.

"The crowd behaved themselves very well. I

hope other supporters follow Manchester City's lead in bringing along inflatable toys to matches. It is a very encouraging sign."

Oldham manager Joe Royle believes that Saturday's trouble-free game proved that soccer does not need the identity cards which the Government will force on the game next season.

Says Royle: "There was a gate of over 19,000 with the majority of them being away fans and there was not an ounce of trouble.

"If an identity card system was in operation

on Saturday many of those fans would still be queueing up now to get in."

VETERAN defender Paul Jones, whose Wigan Athletic debut was blocked on Saturday because he has played in South Africa, could be cleared for tomorrow's Sherpa Van tie at Tranmere.

Jones was a free agent when he went to South Africa last summer and accepted a month's contract with Wigan last week

PFA secretary Gordon Taylor is backing Jones' claim that he did not breach FIFA rules at a meeting with FA officials later today.

With acknowledgements to the "Manchester Evening News".

JUST BANANAS!

GAYLE . . . "we love the fans' antics"

MANCHESTER CITY fans are simply going bananas about the brilliant young side Mel Machin has built.

While the Maine Road men are putting a smile on the face of soccer, their fans are giving everybody a giggle.

At PLYMOUTH'S Home Park one end of the ground was a kaleidoscope of colours as blow-up replicas of giant bananas, pink monkeys and even a fluorescent green shark had everybody laughing.

City's players clearly enjoyed the fun-filled frolics of their supporters who have made a cult of producing a Monty Python approach to following their team.

And City's bunch of banana-waving fans may have started a laugh-a-

By KEN LAWRENCE and KEVIN FRANCIS

minute trend which might just catch on and change the world's image of England's fearsome supporters.

City chairman Peter Swales claimed: "They're putting the smile back into the game—and what they're also doing is kicking the hooligan element right into touch.

Relax

"There hasn't been as much fun in the game since the Mexican Wave did the rounds.

"I just couldn't believe it. After so many years of tension we're now seeing people going to games and laughing and enjoying themselves.

"We all know about the problems we've had in football . . . now hopefully thsi will catch on and bring a bit of the old fun-type atmosphere pack into it."

How the phenomenum started no one knows. But City's Brian Gayle, who got the winner in the 1—0 win, said: "We love the fans waving these things around.

"The idea has caught on like wildfire. It makes us laugh, it lightens the atmosphere and long may it continue.

"Instead of worrying about any trouble we can relax and simply concentrate on our job."

City's current form gives their support every reason to throw their bananas in

the air. The defeat of Plymouth, whom they trounced 6—3 in the Littlewoods Cup three days earlier, was their seventh win in eight games.

Before City's banana republic was paraded the latest in a seemingly unending line of high grade youngsters—17-year-old midfielder Michael Hughes.

With five of Machin's squad already regular England Under-21 players it is clear that City, more than most clubs, want to give youth its head.

Hughes was substituted in the second half and clearly allowed the occasion to overwhelm him. But he has plenty of time to develop as City produce the kind of football which should bring joy to any terracing.

With acknowledgements to the "Daily Star".

THE BANANA PHENOMENON

The 1988-89 season saw City supporters make the headlines for all the right reasons. They were putting the fun back into football by carrying giant inflatables to games and creating a party atmosphere wherever they went. A loyal City fan, Frank Newton, started the banana craze when he took a giant demonstration banana to the first home game of the 1987-88 season. He then took the banana to a few away games including City's local "Derby" at Oldham. The game was played in torrential rain, the fans were drenched; morale was low as Oldham equalised yet the banana was waved throughout the game and brought much needed humour to a depressing day. By the end of the season the banana had been nicknamed "Imre Banana" and a number of smaller bananas had appeared. The last game of the season was at Crystal Palace and *Blue Print,* a new City Fanzine, edited by Mike Kelly, urged supporters to take a blow-up banana. Around fifty bananas made it to Crystal Palace and the scene was set for City supporters to try to enlarge on this the following season.

The supporters seemed to spend all summer looking for new and different inflatables − sharks, Frankensteins, crocodiles, dinosaurs, and many more in addition to the bananas. As the season progressed more and more bananas appeared. When City travelled away the opposition's supporters were stunned when the banana citizens arrived. Newspapers were full of banana stories, City supporters were credited with being the most good natured and fun-loving supporters in the League.

Blue Print − the superb City fanzine − decided to attempt to improve the atmosphere further by trying to organise a fancy dress party for the game at Stoke on Boxing Day. Over 12,000 City supporters travelled to Stoke, with at least 2,000 in fancy dress. The attendance was over 24,000 − Stoke's highest in years. The atmosphere was superb, the supporters were dressed in as many costumes imaginable: priests, soldiers, clowns, and arabs in addition to the usual supply of bananas. The City players joined in the festivities by running on to the pitch, each carrying a giant inflatable banana. These were then tossed into the crowd. Stoke City joined in the fun by welcoming "The Magnificent Supporters from Banana Land". Stoke's receipts for that game were just under £100,000 − a record for a League game at the Victoria Ground. City's following of over 12,000 is believed to be the Club's best following, for a League game, outside of Greater Manchester since the 1968 journey to Newcastle.

The Banana Craze − started by Frank Newton and encouraged by *Blue Print* has been the highlight of the 1980's. Jimmy Greaves and influential figures within football have actively encouraged supporters of all clubs to follow City's lead. During the season, inflatables were seen at most grounds but it is Manchester City's supporters who are nationally known as the TRUE "Banana Citizens".

Carrying giant inflatable bananas, the Manchester City players run out onto the pitch for their game against Leicester. 23,838 spectators watched as City won 1-0. The players are: No. 1-Andy Dibble, No. 4-Brian Gayle, No. 5-Ian Brightwell, No. 7-David White, No. 11-Wayne Biggins. The F.A. Cup game was played on 7th January 1989.

129

BANANA DRAMA

City fans have ball as Machin men hit the top

by RICHARD BOTT
Manchester City 4, Bradford City 0

FOOTBALL'S whackiest army, Manchester City's banana-waving legions, had a ball as two goals apiece from exciting young talents Ian Brightwell and Paul Moulden put their team on the top of the Second Division for the first time this season.

"It's a nice feeling," admitted manager Mel Machin. "We're top of the League because we work hard for each other."

A "purple patch" early on in the second half was enough to edge City into the top spot on goal difference, ahead of Lancashire rivals Blackburn, who beat Ipswich 1—0.

Like so many parties, this one took an age to warm up. For 38 minutes the hosts looked distinctly uncomfortable. Their attacks foundered on Bradford's well-organised defence, reinforced by the use of Peter Jackson as "sweeper," and they should have been punished by Ian Banks and Ian Ormondroyd in turn.

Bradford paid dearly for such gifts.

SAVING HEADER . . . Bradford's Brian Mitchell clears from City's Nigel Gleghorn

With acknowledgements to "The Sunday Express".

OVER THE TOP flies City's Ian Brightwell after opening goal

Right: Scene from the City v. Stoke match on 26th December 1988, when even the Manchester players carried inflatable bananas onto the pitch.

Soccer goes bananas—and it's fun for

MEET the fans who are putting the fun back into football and bringing laughter to terraces once scarred by hooliganism, writes RICHARD BOTT.

If the Sports Minister wants to see the other side of the coin before imposing the membership card scheme, I suggest he takes in a Manchester City game.

An astonishing craze for flying huge plastic bananas has developed among City's followers, home and away.

There is nothing racist in the unlikely trend. A City fan Frank Newton is said to have sparked it off by borrowing a banana to an exhibition at a game at West Ham last season. Wags at City's large travelling contingent immediately nicknamed striker Imre Varadi "Banana." Varadi has left the club, but the craze has grown.

Hundreds of plastic bananas are now paraded at City's matches along with the original king-size version.

Adding to the fun, City fans have also taken to dressing up in costumes such as Frankenstein and Dinosaurs. City captain Steve Redmond told me: "The players are amused by it all. One fan comes to matches dressed up as a fried egg, another has a huge blow-up tennis racket.

"They get the other team's supporters laughing, and it has to be better for the game than seeing them at each other's throats."

The club is cashing in, too. Commercial manager Phil Critchely says: "The banana craze was mentioned by a shareholder at the annual meeting and we were able to tell him we had persuaded a major banana supplier to take an advertising board at Maine Road."

CRAZY GANG . . . the Maine Road faithful make merry at their banana party

With acknowledgements to "The Sunday Express".

PUTTING FUN BACK INTO SOCCER

The banana boffin!

Banana boffin Frank Newton, all ready for take-off

Picture: JOHN WARDAUGH

By JOHN BEAN

THE football boffin behind Manchester City's Bananarama craze isn't your usual terrace type.

Frank Newton, who introduced the giant inflatable fruit to the place, is an assistant computer analyst who took up his station at Maine Road while studying for a degree at Manchester University.

"It all started at the beginning of last season. Everyone was pig sick after City's relegation and I thought it was time to bring some fun back into the game," says Frank.

Contrast

"It seems the idea has worked. You couldn't get a much happier place than a spot in City's Kippax Stand these days."

Newton calculates that around 3,000 inflatables—bananas, dinosaurs, Frankenstein monsters, fried eggs, paddling pools—wobble joyfully when City get a goal at home these days.

Away, he can virtually guarantee 1,000 air-filled emblems of a cult that is

showing signs of bouncing through the League.

"It would be marvellous if it did. It's all a big contrast to the time I got a 5ft. 6ins. plastic banana off a pal and trundled it along to City's first home game against Plymouth last season.

"It was a hot day. Suddenly my shirt was off... and on the banana. Then I painted a face on it. Soon afterwards I took the banana into a knot of City fans at West Brom.

"Someone shouted 'It's Imre Banana'—and the association with Imre Varadi, the player, was born.

"One or two other fans started to take inflatables on to the terraces. But the thing really took off in response to an appeal in City's fan magazine 'Blue Print' to spread the cult across the terraces.

Where will it end? Frank Newton, who has already introduced 10-month-old daughter Alice to Maine Road, doesn't know. But I suspect it will take a lot of deflating.

With acknowledgements
to the "Daily Express".

Ian Scott, the City substitute for the match against Leicester, throws his banana into the main stand prior to the game. He was brought on as substitute in the 50th minute of the Cup Tie on 7th January 1989. Scott played in City's Youth Team, which won the F.A. Youth Cup in 1986, and made his senior team debut on 15th August 1987.

EXPRESS POSTLINE

COMPILED BY KEITH DONNELLY

This bunch deserve the Final taste

BANANARAMA ... Maine Road style

£25 LETTER

AN enterprising Manchester market trader had the following sign over his bananas: "Munch a bunch at Maine Road on Saturday."

I asked if he would be having any Cup Final tickets and he said: "Keep all the skins, they count as vouchers." Yes, the fun is back in football thanks to the wonderful Manchester City fans.

Wouldn't it be a magnificent reward if we could see their colourful hoardes at Wembley this coming May?

J PRINCE, Langley Estate, Manchester.

Turn the place into a Banana Republic, they would!

Festive frolics as fans go bananas

With acknowledgements to the "Evening Sentinel".

More than 12,000 Manchester City supporters brought a carnival atmosphere to the Victoria ground for the match against Stoke City on 26th December 1988. Stoke won 3-1 in front of a total crowd of 24,056.

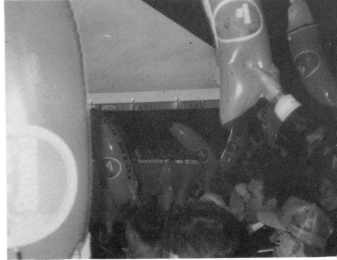

MANCHESTER CITY MANAGERS

Listed below are all the men who have managed City since the team entered the League in 1892 as Ardwick A.F.C.

1889-93	Lawrence Furniss	1932-46	Wilf Wild	1973-74	Ron Saunders
1893-95	Joshua Parlby	1946-47	Sam Cowan	1974-79	Tony Book
1895-02	Sam Ormerod	1947-50	Jock Thomson	1979-80	Malcolm Allison
1902-06	Tom Maley	1950-63	Les McDowall	1980-83	John Bond
1906-12	Harry Newbould	1963-65	George Poyser	1983	John Benson
1912-24	Ernest Mangnall	1965-72	Joe Mercer, OBE	1983-86	Billy McNeill, MBE
1924-26	David Ashworth	1972-73	Malcolm Allison	1986-87	Jimmy Frizzell
1926-32	Peter Hodge	1973	John Hart	1987	Mel Machin

MAINE ROAD FACTS

Highest Attendance: 84,569 v. Stoke, F.A. Cup 6th Round, 3rd March 1934.
Highest League Attendance: 77,582 v. Arsenal, Division One, 23rd February 1935.
Highest League Cup Attendance: 55,799 v. Manchester United, 19th November 1969.
Highest Manchester "Derby" Attendance: 77,000, Division One, 20th September 1947 and 7th April 1948.
Lowest League Attendance: 8,015 v. Swindon, Division Two, 16th January 1965.
Manchester United's highest and lowest attendances were both recorded at Maine Road.
Highest: 82,950 v. Arsenal, Division One, 17th January 1948. *Record crowd for a League game.*
Lowest: 7,800 v. Stoke, Division One, 5th February 1947.

The record attendance for any midweek F.A. Cup game is 80,407 at Maine Road for the Semi-Final Replay between Derby County and Birmingham City on 28th March 1946.

CITY v. UNITED

The first game between the two clubs was on 12th November 1881 when St. Mark's, West Gorton (City) visited North Road to play Newton Heath (United). St. Mark's lost the game 3-0, but won the return match 2-1, in March 1882, at the Kirkmanshulme Cricket Club Ground. Below is a full record of all Derby games:

	Played	Won	Drawn	Lost	Goals For	Against
Football League	110	31	39	40	150	155
F.A. Cup	5	2	0	3	6	9
League Cup	4	2	1	1	8	4
Charity Shield	1	0	0	1	0	1
Football Alliance	2	0	1	1	3	5
F.L. Jubilee Games	2	1	1	0	3	2
Manchester & Salford Cup	1	0	0	1	2	5
Healey Cup	2	2	0	0	6	3
Benefit Matches	2	1	0	1	5	5
Testimonials	6	4	0	2	14	11
Friendlies	36	10	7	19	48	69
League & W.W.1 Cup Games	16	9	3	4	26	18
League and W.W.2 Cup Games	25	12	4	9	47	42
Manchester Cup	25	9	3	13	40	50
Lancashire Cup	9	4	1	4	12	18
Manchester Tournament	1	0	0	1	1	3
Total	247	87	60	100	371	397

INTERESTING FACTS

The 1967 F.A. Amateur Cup Final replay was held at Maine Road, when Enfield beat Skelmersdale 3-0 before a crowd of 55,388.

* * *

City's appearance record is held by Alan Oakes, who made a total of 665 appearances, and a further 3 as substitute, between 1959 and 1976.

* * *

In 1977 Manchester City Council named a number of Streets after former City stars: Horace Barnes Close, Eric Brook Close, Tommy Browell Close, Sammy Cookson Close, Sam Cowan Close, Billy Meredith Close, Fred Tilson Close and Max Woosnam Walk. These Streets are in an area between Claremont Road, Maine Road, Great Western Street and Princess Road.

* * *

S.B. Ashworth was one of only three amateur players to have won an F.A. Cup Winners' Medal during the 20th century. He played for city during the 1904 Final. He had played in the Amateur Cup Final the previous year for Oxford City.

OLDHAM LADIES v. MANCHESTER CITY LADIES
At Boundary Park
OLDHAM . . . 1 v. MANCHESTER CITY . . . 4
City scorers: Donna Haynes 2; Heidi Ward 2
An outstanding performance from City in this their first match of the season.
Notable performances for City, Haynes and Ward for all round work, Felton — who emerged as mid-field playmaker, Burnett—good old fashioned wing play and Mather, cool and calm at the back.

City team: M. Flynn, R. Foxwell, T. Slack, M. Cox, M. Mather, L. Burnett, K. Thomson, L. Felton (Capt.), H. Ward, D. Haynes, A. Hewnelt: Subs: C. Morrison, M. Braddock, D. Davies, A. Marland, D. Darbyshire, D. Crystal, B. Emerson.

ATTENDANCE DETAILS
The following are Manchester City's average attendance figures for every league season. Figures prior to 1946 are rounded to the nearest thousand and have been based on newspaper reports of the period which were often inaccurate and usually guessed by the reporters.

1892-93	3,000*	**1914-15**	21,000	**1946-47**	38,195	**1967-68**	37,214
1893-94	4,000*	**1919-20**	25,000	**1947-48**	37,435	**1968-69**	33,725
1894-95	6,000	**1920-21**	31,000	**1948-49**	35,772	**1969-70**	33,949
1895-96	10,000	**1921-22**	25,000	**1949-50**	39,302	**1970-71**	31,044
1896-97	8,000	**1922-23**	24,000	**1950-51**	34,753	**1971-72**	38,707
1897-98	8,000	**1923-24**	27,000	**1951-52**	37,585	**1972-73**	32,271
1898-99	10,000	**1924-25**	29,000	**1952-53**	35,219	**1973-74**	30,650
1899-00	16,000	**1925-26**	32,000	**1953-54**	30,042	**1974-75**	32,899
1900-01	17,000	**1926-27**	28,000	**1954-55**	35,165	**1975-76**	34,284
1901-02	17,000	**1927-28**	36,000	**1955-56**	32,587	**1976-77**	40,053
1902-03	16,000	**1928-29**	33,000	**1956-57**	30,005	**1977-78**	41,686
1903-04	20,000	**1929-30**	33,000	**1957-58**	32,759	**1978-79**	36,216
1904-05	20,000	**1930-31**	25,000	**1958-59**	32,564	**1979-80**	35,244
1905-06	18,000	**1931-32**	23,000	**1959-60**	36,250	**1980-81**	33,535
1906-07	22,000	**1932-33**	23,000	**1960-61**	28,611	**1981-82**	33,016
1907-08	23,000	**1933-34**	28,000	**1961-62**	25,626	**1982-83**	26,788
1908-09	20,000	**1934-35**	33,000	**1962-63**	24,655	**1983-84**	24,677
1909-10	16,000	**1935-36**	33,000	**1963-64**	18,200	**1984-85**	22,284
1910-11	26,000	**1936-37**	34,000	**1964-65**	14,753	**1985-86**	24,219
1911-12	22,000	**1937-38**	32,000	**1965-66**	27,739	**1986-87**	22,324
1912-13	24,000	**1938-39**	29,000	**1966-67**	30,735	**1987-88**	19,468
1913-14	27,000						

*As Ardwick A.F.C.